JAILS, HOSPITALS & HIP-HOP

AND

SOME PEOPLE

JAILS, HOSPITALS & HIP-HOP

AND

SOME PEOPLE

DANNY HOCH

Peace & Justice
Danny Hoch

VILLARD NEW YORK

Some People was originally created in 1993 and a revised version was published in 1998 by Caseroc Productions c/o Washington Square Arts, New York.

Library of Congress Cataloging-in-Publication Data
Hoch, Danny.
Jails, hospitals & hip-hop and some people / Danny Hoch.
p. cm.
ISBN 0-375-75339-7
1. United States—Social conditions—20th century—Drama.
2. Ethnic groups—United States—Drama. 3. Performance art.
4. Monologues. I. Title.
PS3558.033695J35 1998
812'.54—dc21 98-35752

Random House website address: www.randomhouse.com

Printed in the United States of America

BVG 01

BOOK DESIGN BY BARBARA M. BACHMAN

For my mother
. . . who taught me
how to really listen

ACKNOWLEDGMENTS

THERE ARE MANY PEOPLE TO THANK, without whose support, advice, and sweat this work would not have been possible. To Jo Bonney, my director, dramaturg, and friend, who made me write down the oral language spewing from my mouthpiece. You see theatre so clearly and I'm in a fog. Thank you for your vision and patience while I sat in my house in Brooklyn buggin' out.

Mad heartfelt thank-yous and good-lookin'-outs to: JT Rogers, Gus Reyes, Rebecca Ashley, and the Next Stage Company, who were there with me in a freezing Gas Station hanging lights and sticking posters all over Ave. B; Greg Freelon, David Ellis, Mark Russell, Alison Loubel, Lynn Moffat, Dave Overcamp, Sarah Sidman, Performance Space 122, Dominick Balletta, Andrea Smith, Florian Schattauer, Performance Associates, the Jerome Foundation, Shelby Jiggetts-Tivony, Morgan Jenness, George Wolfe, the Joseph Papp Public Theatre, the Solo Mio Festival in San Francisco, the Baltimore Theatre Project, William McLaughlin, David Campbell, Jon Rubin, Brigett Potter, Robert Small, John Fortenberry, Greg Gattuso, Paula Court, Dona Ann McAdams, Paula Scher, Nchito, Yaurelita, Brooklyn-Queens Nation, Leah Nelson, Greg Hubbard, Gwendolen Hardwick, NYU's Creative Arts Team, Peter Askin, Flaco Navaja, Washington Square Arts (Kathie Russo and Mary Shimkin), Lindsay Porter, Scott Yoselow, James Morrison, Tom D'Ambrosio, Nancy Losey, Garth Belcon, New York State Council on the Arts, Berkeley Repertory Theatre (Tony Taccone, Susie Medak, Tony Kelly, Cliff Mayotte), Ted Striggles, Kiku Yamaguchi (you busted your ass), Clyde Valentin, Stress Publishing, Peter Hagan, Dan Greenberg, Bruce Tracy, and Villard Books.

Most important, there would be no performance without you, the audience. There are tons of you (and you know who you are) who keep coming to my workshops, my works-in-progress, and my finished shows. You have helped this work develop. You are this performance! Without you, plain and simple, there is no show. Thank you.

ONE LOVE.

CONTENTS

INTRODUCTION

PEACE TO MY AUDIENCE!

Welcome to my book. Two shows: *Jails, Hospitals & Hip-Hop* and *Some People.* It's been a while gettin' to this point. I was born in 1970, a third-generation New Yorker lucky enough to grow up during the birth of Hip-Hop culture in a towering brick and asphalt outer-borough neighborhood, where there was no racial majority or minority. I trained as an actor, to play everything from Molière to Tennessee Williams to Sam Shepard to Samuel Beckett to Shakespeare, even Neil Simon. It was invaluable, and probably saved my life from some of my teenage ill-street escapades.

There was one problem. Although my teachers were wonderful and my training was intense, I was being trained to drop the languages I grew up with. In order to be a "successful" actor, I was supposed to forget all of the rich language that was my whole cultural foundation. It was mapped out for me to be in Broadway or off-Broadway shows, movies, or TV shows that had nothing to do with the people or stories from my community, or even my generation. Tom Stoppard and Harold Pinter don't write about Grandmaster Flash or disco bar-mitzvahs or mofongo. To put it Brooklyn style: *Showboat* and *Sideshow* ain't don't got nothin' to do with my life. I had mad beef with this situation.

Theatre is *about* language. Oral, physical, and spiritual language, and that's it. If I can't relate to the universality of the character's language; if I'm excluded by the abstraction of the art taking place; if I live in Brooklyn and all I get to see is *Arcadia, Home Improvement, The English Patient,* and *Martin,* then what's the point? There is no pathos, no catharsis whatsoever, in the intellectual and anti-intellectual bullshit that calls itself art and entertainment. We sit there thinking about the holes in our socks. Or maybe we laugh or cry. But all we're permitted to do is laugh and cry at the characters, not at ourselves. We sit passively entertained instead of actively engaged.

I wanted no part of this theatre. Somewhere around when I was eighteen, I decided to make my own theatre. All of the stories, voices, and characters that *I* felt were important I put onstage. I "wrote" it all orally in front of audiences. The characters were not confined to a page. They were alive, allowed to breathe, to go wherever they wanted. I called it structured improvisation. Eventually I would keep the good stuff and get rid of the bad stuff, and boom—I had a show. It was called *Pot Melting,* and the few thousand people who saw it back in the early 1990s will remember that it changed a bit from show to show, because I never really wrote down any of the dozen characters that I created. It was oral theatre the ancient way, but with modern themes and today's language.

I had the same approach to *Some People,* although this time I worked with a director, Jo Bonney. I needed someone with an outside eye. I was reluctant to do this for many reasons. Usually what directors do is take a script, digest it, interpret it, and stage it according to their personal, inspired "artistic vision." But how do you collaborate when it's *your* vision? How do you direct oral language? How do you help shape voices that already have their own distinct shapes? How do you direct something that is improvised?

I found out very quickly, it didn't matter that my director couldn't tell the difference between Jamaican and Trinidadian patois or Cuban and Dominican Spanish. What was important was that she understood how the social function of theatre operates: that we are really blue-collar workers who happen to manufacture popular, provocative, educational entertainment. She also understood the relationship between the solo actor and the audience, a relationship that is often looked at not as theatre but as stand-up comedy (an entirely different dynamic). What theatre director knows how to stage a play with a cast of one? This one did.

The first thing she did was make me actually write down what happened orally onstage and look at it. I was horrified. I always felt that sitting and writing is more of an intellectual, almost mathematical way of creating, as opposed to creating in front of an audience, which is purely visceral. But okay, I submit. There's something to be said for writing things down. For the first time, I actually saw what I was saying—dramaturgically. This helped me shape a better "structure" to work from while I was onstage. Basically, it refined the visceral fragmented storytelling riffs into clarified visceral stories that *sounded* like riffs.

Solo theatre is actually something very ancient. It predates the Roman and Greek theatrical histories and can be found in the indigenous theatres of Africa, Asia, and the Americas (before European colonialism). When the French were colonizing Africa, they used the word *griot* to describe the various solo performers they encountered: people who used drama, comedy, pantomime, storytelling, dance, music, possession, and masks to create community performance. The griots reflected, celebrated, reconstructed, and questioned the community. In other words—pure unfiltered theatre. They were shamans, teachers, preachers, actors, and social critics, all in one.

In the United States, because of our young sense of cultural history, we are not terribly familiar with solo theatre. We are, however, accustomed to stand-up comedians, talk show hosts, mimes, magicians, politicians, rabbis, and priests. Well, I wanted to be an urban griot for the communities of urban North America.

A few people think I am some anthropological/theatrical case-study guy. But I don't tape-record or interview people to then play them onstage. This is my world! These are my inner monologues, layered composites of stories and voices from me, my family, my neighborhood, my people. I think all the hoopla about my work comes from people simply not being accustomed to seeing traditionally peripheral characters placed center stage. Well, these characters are center stage in *my* world.

Contrary to what many purveyors of theatre would have us think, North America isn't just people who live near strip malls in two-story houses somewhere in the suburbs. This nation is teeming with communities where rich and middle-class white people are *not* at the center; yet we see who is deemed deserving of our stage time.

I often wonder if my skin were darker, or if I couldn't flip my linguistics during meetings to sound "businesslike and un-threatening" (I swear somebody said that to me), if I would have had the success I've had with these two shows. Was I a "safe in" to the "disenfranchised voices of America" for the rich and middle class? Maybe. This country is some wild shit.

A lot of Hollywood people have come to my shows, and I was offered several opportunities to write and act in television and film. Seeing them happen was another story. I'm actually not surprised at the resistance I've come up against in the entertainment/media/propaganda industry when trying to get three-dimensional poor characters and non-Eurocentric characters into mainstream storylines. I just never imagined that producers and publishers and studio executives would blatantly say things like, "People don't want to watch Puerto Ricans" or "America is mostly white people, you don't want to disinterest them" or "It's funnier with the black accent" (what is a black accent?), or "You can't have a piece entirely in Spanish, who's gonna get it?" Wow, right? Shit is real out there.

Although this is a book of monologues, these are also two plays. And although I wrote each play down on paper (like my director told me to), the characters have evolved over the course of many performances. Even as *Some People* opened at P.S. 122, ran at the Public Theatre, and toured, it changed. This edition is based on the last round of shows I did in 1996, and it contains the full, uncut monologues that appeared in the 1995 HBO special, as well as three other pieces from the original live show that didn't make it to HBO: "Madman," "Al Capón," and "Flex." *Jails, Hospitals & Hip-Hop* is based on the last round of shows in New York in 1998.

I consider it a privilege having grown up in New York City during Hip-Hop's infancy, writing graffiti on trains, b-boying (breakdancing), and rapping. I might be an actor, writer, and teacher, but Hip-Hop formed my language and my entire worldview. It influences my theatre, whether the subject matter is Hip-Hop or not. I could be doing a piece about religion or war, and Hip-Hop would still inform the way I see it. I also spent time doing theatre on Riker's Island and in various borough detention centers and prisons, and was profoundly affected by the vast numbers of people whose lives are dependent on, and governed by, the prison industrial complex. It is colossal. It's so colossal, it makes Ford Motor Company look like a small business.

My mother worked as a speech pathologist in a hospital in the Bronx. I spent some of my childhood there, watching her teach people how to reclaim language. People who were in car accidents. People who were quadriplegics from police gunshot wounds. There was a kid who was sitting in a school bus on his way home while the landlords were burning the Bronx for tax write-offs. He got hit in the head with a brick while people were looting and protesting. Every word is now a jewel more precious than a thousand diamonds.

As rappers don themselves with Italian mafia names; as urban youth clothe themselves with expensive sailing, skiing, camping, and hiking apparel and suburban youth copy the fashions, trying to be like the urban youth (who no doubt sail, ski, and camp in their spare time); as we all co-opt each other's cultures and modes of speech and try so hard to be like one another, Hip-Hop backspins in irony, trying to make sense of the high school dropout in

Brooklyn who talks of black power while deciding which Tommy Hilfiger shirt to wear with his Nikes (as if dressing like a sailor is going to keep him from being harassed by the police), or of the business college freshman in North Carolina who spray-paints THUG LIFE on the barn in his father's tobacco field during spring break. Because let's face it, thug life is far more attractive and entertaining than business college life. It's just cooler to be the oppressed than the oppressor. Who wants to be the oppressor? Shit, not me.

Even with all the negative representations of Hip-Hop that are thrust in our faces every day (as if only Hip-Hop can be violent and misogynistic); even though Hip-Hop, like every culture of resistance in this country, has been co-opted and commodified to sell fast food, beer, liquor, and soda; there still exists in Hip-Hop a strong voice of resistance, questioning, and demand for change that can't be stopped. Fuck the Internet—Hip-Hop is the future of language and culture in the multicultural society. It crosses all lines of color, race, economics, nationality, and gender, and Hip-Hop still has something to say.

While New York's Hot 97 Radio proclaims, "Hip-Hop Rules the World," suit-clad men in Washington decide whether or not to bomb Iraq, starve Cuba and Africa, and lock up our youth. As Mayor Rudolph Giuliani eliminates the Department of Youth Services in a city with two million youths, and as he shuts schools and hospitals, opens jails, and donates millions to Wall Street in the same breath, I dedicate *Jails, Hospitals & Hip-Hop and Some People* to the young people of New York City. We have always resisted the regular, done our own thing, and looked fly doing it. Spit ill lyrics to ruffle the feathers of devils.

Flip divine styles to uplift your community. Spin wild beats to shift the earth's position. Use Hip-Hop as your weapon, education as your rock, and don't stop till the break of dawn.

PEACE OUT . . .

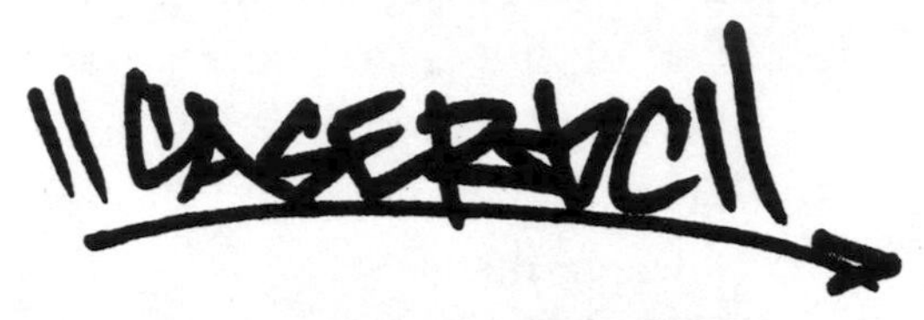

A.K.A. DANNY HOCH
BROOKLYN, NEW YORK
AUGUST 1998

A NEW SOLO SHOW BY

DANNY HOCH

JAILS HOSPITALS HIP-HOP

Developed & Directed by Jo Bonney

NOW THROUGH JUNE 27th ONLY!

Tickets $10, $25

Performance Space 122 | 150 1st Ave. at E.9th St., NYC | 212-477-5288

PAULA COURT

The set consists of two file cabinets, a bench, and a chair. Everything looks bureaucratic and government issued.

The only costumes for the characters are an occasional hat or shirt that are thrown into a file drawer when finished.

MESSAGE TO THE BLUNTMAN

[PROLOGUE]

FORTIES, BLUNTS, HO'S. Glocks and Tecs
You got your *X* cap but I got you powerless

Forties, Blunts, Ho's. Glocks and Tecs
You got your Tommy Hil but I got you
powerless

People be like shut the hell up when I talk
Like I shouldn't be talkin' "black," even though
I'm from New York

But what's that? A color, a race, or a state of
mind?
A class of people? A culture, is it a rhyme?

If so, then what the hell am I, you might be
sayin'?
Well, see if you could follow this flow, 'cause I
ain't playin'

Ya see, I ain't ya average twenty-something
grunge type of slacker
I'm not your herb flavor-of-the-month, I ain't
no cracker

An actor? Come on now, you know you wanna ask me
I'll use my skin privileges to flag you down a taxi

But I could act mad type of rough to flex my muscle
I'm also from the seventies so I could do the Hustle

I been to Riker's Island, did crimes that was wrong
Smoked Blunts and drank Forties 'fore Kriss Kross was born!

That's true. But so what. I know I ain't "that" to you
But I can take your culture; soup it up, and sell it back to you

And I can sell crack to you and smack to you if you let me
I'm the president, the press, and your paycheck, you sweat me

You never even met me or can fathom my derision
You try to buck my system, son, I'll lock yo ass in prison

'Cause that's my mission, profit in my pocket, I clock it
I got billions invested in jails, you can't stop it

I'm political, I laugh at all this anti-Semitical
It makes you look weak when you try to be critical

And I laugh at all these rap videos with these guns
and Ho's
While you strike the roughneck pose, I pick my
nose

And flick it on ya, ya goner, no need to warn ya
I got mad seats in government from Bronx to
California

And I got the National Guard and plus the Navy,
Army, Air Force, son, I got *niggers* paid to save me

If it ever really gets to that but I doubt it
'Cause these dollars that I print got your mind
clouded

A kid steps on your sneakers and you beef with no
hesitation
But you never got beef with my legislation or my
TV station

This is my game, I can't lose
When I wanna see the score I just turn on my
news

And see you got my Glock and my Tec, aimed at
your man neck
I got you in check and you still give me respect

Ha. That's real funny, Mister Money
Mister Cash Loot Blunts Ho's, Mister Dummy

Mister Car Cellular Phone, Mister Junk
You think you got props, you got jack, you the
punk

This revolution lookin' like junk, and it sunk
With all the *X* caps that I sold you out my trunk

You bought my revolution and you wear it on
your head
And then you be talkin' 'bout, Yeah, I'ma shoot
you dead!

Who you supposed to be scarin', brother?
You ain't scarin' me, but you scarin' your mother

So keep buyin' this fly revolution that I'm sellin'
How much gee's I'll make off you herbs, yo ain't
no tellin'

Keep buyin' my Philly Blunt shirts and my hats
Keep buyin' my Forties, and keep buyin' them
Gats

And I'll keep buyin' time with the cash that you
spend
We could hang out, I'll even call you my friend

And we can watch this televised revolution that
you're missin'
On the commercials that's between Rush
Limbaugh and *The Simpsons*

What's the moral of this limerick that I kicked?
If you missed it, well maybe your head is thick

Or maybe your ass is too high from the Blunts
That's too bad, 'cause revolution only happens
once

Forties, Blunts, Ho's. Glocks and Tecs
You got your *X* cap but I got you power . . . less

Forties, Blunts, Ho's. Glocks and Tecs
You got your Tommy Hil and your Lex . . . but
what's next?

PAULA COURT

BRONX

[A man in his mid-twenties loiters in a hallway of the C-74 building on Riker's Island, New York City. He conversates with a new inmate.]

.....**REALLY? THAT'S MESSED UP, MAN.** I hear you. .....Yeah. .....Wow. Hey yo, do me a favor? Take a walk with me for one second? I gotta get a toothbrush. Just take a walk with me to get a toothbrush for one second. [They walk.] But for real, man, if I was you, I would talk to your lawyer and tell him that you wanna plea bargain. 'Cause even though you was just an accomplice, if you plead not guilty, and it goes to trial, they could decide to make it a first-degree felony against *you,* and that's it. I'm sayin', whatever, even if you not an accomplice, whatever, bee, I wasn't there, I ain't sayin' you did nothin', man. I mean, I just met you yesterday. But especially, 'cause you're black. . . . I mean . . . are you black? .....Oh, I wasn't sure, I thought you might be, whatever. Still, just plead guilty, guilty, guilty. I seen it happen before. Even if you didn't do it. Otherwise they start makin' deals with all your peoples, make it look like you're the one that pioneered the whole shit. Then they get you for conspiracy when you was just an accomplice—or you just happened to be there, like I said I wasn't there, I ain't sayin' you did nothin'.

[He calls an officer.] On the gate! On the gate! Officer on the gate! .....Nah, to inmate services—for a toothbrush, they took his toothbrush in the dorm. Right? Right, they took your toothbrush in the dorm? They took his toothbrush in the dorm! .....That's my ID card right there. Show him your ID card, pa. .....So we'll wait right here then. Damn, where we going? Right?

[Back to the guy] I'm tellin' you, if I was you, I would just say guilty, take the bid, do your little one-to-three, whatever, politic, you know. Me, I got different problems, man. See, I try to do the right thing, they lock me up. Giuliani's like, "Oh, people on welfare are lazy." I'm tryin' not to be on that shit. I'm workin', right? I'm in Fordham Road. I'm sellin' Bart Simpson T-shirts, and um, what you call it—O. J. Simpson T-shirts, right? This cop come up, arrest me 'cause I don't got a license. I'm not selling drugs! I'm not selling drugs! I'm selling Bart Simpson T-shirts, O. J. Simpson T-shirts. That's work, man. You think that shit is easy? That shit is hard, man, I don't even wanna go into it. .....Nah, but that's illegal? They said it's illegal. You know, I'm tryin' to do right in my life, man. I wanna be a entrepreneur, or whatever you call it. You know if I was that little girl that they show on TV in that commercial selling lemonade in front of her house, you think the cop gonna arrest *her?* Nah-ah! Nah-ah! But see, if you think about it, the little girl, she's a entrepreneur, just like me. She's a businesswoman. She got—what you call it?—overhead. She gotta get her sugar, her lemons, her cups, she makes her stand, then she stand outside all day. Me? I got my shirts, my stand, I stand outside all day. But you know if that cop see her in front of her house with her little white picket fence or whatever, he'd be like, "Oh . . ." —all jolly and shit—"that's so cute, lemme get a lemonade, sweetheart?" Right? And then he'd drink his lemonade and then he'd say, "Mm, tasty . . . whatever whatever." Then he leave. Then he go beat up some people. Then he go home and fuck his wife, and feel like, it's not really such a bad day today. God bless America, right? But he see me in Fordham Road? Nah-ah, different story. He step to me, "Hey you! Where's your fucking license?" He gonna say, "Where's your fucking license" to the little girl? Nah-ah! Nah-ah! See, what is it, he don't care if I got a license or I don't got a license.

He don't like the way I look. I live in 163rd Street, I got a certain look. People in Park Avenue, *they* got a certain look. But the cop gonna see somebody from Park Avenue or Tribeca, hauling three kilos of cocaine to their girlfriend's house, on their designer fucking Rollerblades or whatever, he's not gonna get disturbed by their look. He'll say, "Hey, how are you? Have a donut. Okey-dokey, buddy." Or whatever. But then he see somebody that appears—I don't even know—*unprofessional,* or whatever, he automatic think criminal.

So this cop, he gets out the car all with his cop shit. But see, he had sunglasses, so when he look at me first from the car, I look darker. When he get out, he get *confused.* 'Cause if you put me next to the cop, I'm whiter than the cop. He start askin' me, "What are you? What are you?" I say, "That's not your business, you wanna buy a shirt?" Then he knock over all my shit in the street, the shirts is dirty. Now I have dirty products. I have to pay for that shit. And peoples is laughin' at me, man.

Next thing, he throw me down in the ground, he got his nightstick in my back, with the spit and the gum from the sidewalk is in my face and shit. He say, "What are you, what are you?!! Are you Puerto Rican, are you

Puerto Rican?" I say, "Nah, I'm not Puerto Rican yo, I'm selling Bart Simpson, O. J. Simpson T-shirts, what's the problem officer?" But see, he wanna know, what am I? I mean, my color is white like Bill Clinton, but that's not good enough for him, you know, in the way that I'm speaking, or I don't even know. He got a complex, he needs to see a therapist 'cause he's confused. Then, he look at the T-shirts, and he get more confused. 'Cause he don't know who's Bart Simpson. He knows Bart Simpson is Bart Simpson, but he don't know Bart Simpson is Dominican, Jewish, Greek, Puerto Rican? What is he? He don't know, but he know that Bart Simpson and O. J. Simpson make more money than *him,* so he feel threatened. Then the cop look at me, and he see somebody that's a entrepreneur, that's trying to start a business from nothing, that I'm busting my ass. He see that I have the possibility to better my situation. That I have the opportunity to increase my status, or whatever you call it. And then he looks at himself, and he sees that he's just a *servant* and that's it. Even if he turn captain, lieutenant, police chief, whatever, he's just a servant and that's all he *gonna* be. . . . So he feel threatened. And 'cause he feel threaten, that day he gonna decide capitalism is illegal. And 'cause I got a prior felony on my record, they put me in here. [To another guy] You got a cigarette?

[Back to guy number one] See, if you analyze it with the little girl and the lemonade, that's supposed to be America, right? That you could stand outside your house and sell whatever. If that's not true that you could do that, don't advertise it then. Don't put it in the TV, you know? To be honest with you, I seen that commercial, I got inspired by that shit. I said yo, shit ain't really that bad, I got chances and shit. Now I'm in fucking jail, bro. I feel like *suing* them lemonade motherfuckers, man. Or suing somebody. .....For false advertising. .....I *know* I wasn't selling lemonade, that's not the—Hey yo, shut up, bro. I didn't really ask you to respond and shit, damn.

[To another guy] You got a light? [Back to guy number one] .....Nah, they arrested me a month ago, I ain't even had a hearing, nothing. First they had me in C-73, I was there for two weeks, but I got in a fight, this guy tried to cut me. Motherfucker tried to assassinate me right in the TV room and shit, 'cause I wanna change the channel in the TV. So they transferred me to 74, lock me here. .....Nah, this kid tried to step to me 'cause I tried to get them to watch something else, man. They sitting there for two weeks watching that Tonya Hardy/Nancy Kardigan shit. How you gonna tell me that shit interests you, man? You don't even know what's figure-skating, I told them, man. What the fuck is that? That concerns you? Ice-skating got nothing to do with my life. Once my mother took me ice-skating to Rockefeller Center when I was three years old, I fell in my ass and I cried, I said, "What's this shit? A sport?" Now I'm in jail and I sit there every day, I have to watch that shit. That shit is punishment for real, man.

I don't give a fuck about one girl don't want the other girl to win the World Ice Medal, then she gonna start scheming and get some kid with a golf club to hit her in the fucking knee. That shit is cartoons, man. They in there debating over that shit, fighting. "She did it!" "No, she didn't do it!" I told them, "You in jail, man, fight over your shoes or some shit!" Goddammit. But you know what is it? I figured it out. It's that people like to see these smiling cornflake-type women fucking each other up. 'Cause if you think about it, you never really see, or you rarely see, nah, you might see like in a soap opera or some shit. Like, one lady's like, "Oh, I'm gonna take her man, or I'm gonna stab that bitch, or poison her tea . . ." or whatever. But in real life, they're all sitting around the sofa drinking ginger ale and shit. So when it happens in real life, people eat that shit up. They're like, "What?! Two white ladies fighting? Where?!" and shit. They pay money to see that shit. In cable. In pay-per-view.

Every single day for four months, in the news with that. Right? .....Who you trying to play? You know you was watching. But see, they make that ice-skating/golf-club bullshit the number one story. They try to make you think that that's the most important shit that you should be concerned about, so that you forget, they try to distract you, to make you ignore, from that you can't feed your kid and shit, that you can't fulfill your dreams 'cause people won't hire you 'cause you got a felony on your record. Fuck that, I had to change the channel, man. .....Nah, this kid wanna act hardrock with me, pull a razor. Pssh. I cut him before he cut me. .....Nah, he wanna force me to act like a criminal. I ain't in here 'cause I'm a criminal. I'm in here 'cause I'm poor, that's why I'm in here!

[To the officer] .....Huh? A toothbrush. .....Yeah. That's what we're waiting for. [To guy number one] Go get your toothbrush. .....Nah, he ain't gonna let me. He ain't gonna let me. Yo, see if you could get two. . . . Tell 'em they took two . . .

PAULA COURT

FLIP

[Some really bad West Coast rap plays in the background. A white teenager stands in front of his mirror trying different positions with the baseball cap on his head, attempting the thug look. He bounces around the stage and raps to an imaginary concert crowd, trying out various physicalities that he's seen on MTV and BET.]

I BE THE *F* TO THE *L* TO THE *I* TO THE *P*
Destroyin' motherfuckers, yeah, that's my
hobby
Any sucker emcee wanna come test me
I put a bullet in yo ass with my fuckin' Uzi

Niggas get killed tryin' to bite my stee
My main nigga Trev, pass the for-tee
So I could get loose and blow niggas out the
frame
Don't even try to trip because Flip be my name

Yeah . . . Fuck the food stamps and the welfare
change
I'm tryin' to get a Pathfinder plus a Range—

[He is interrupted by his mother's voice. He walks to his door and yells.] What?! I took the bottles to the store already! I left the change on the counter! I put it on top of the coupons! Next to the microwave. .....That's where I put it. .....Then quit botherin' me then! Damn. [He goes back to the mirror and regroups.]

I'm tryin' to get a Pathfinder plus a Range—
. . . Rover . . . with a house in France filled with
ho's
Michael-Jordan-type stock portfolios . . .

Vanilla Ice, he could suck my fuckin' dick
That fool Bryant Gumbel makes me fuckin' sick
Sittin' at his desk talkin' mad fuckin' shit
Lala la lala that shit is fuckin' bull*shit*!

My niggas is in the front, while you be in the back
Fuck bein' white, word up, dude, I'm black
I'm only seventeen but my shit still thump
And by the time I'm eighteen I'll be chillin' with
Donald Trump
[He freezes in a snapshot gangsta thug pose.] Yeah, man.

Thank you, thank you. Thank you, all my fans. Flip-Dogg on the m-i-c. What you thought it was, fool? You knowhamsayin'? Biotch! Yeah, man. Thank you, thank you. [He gestures behind him.] Oh thanks, Jay. Thanks a lot, Jay. Ya little fucker. [He trots around a little bit more, then suddenly bursts into a thug fantasy.]

I thought I said a gee! This ain't no gee, nigga! .....What?! You tryin' to be slick with me? I'ma blast you. *Blaow!* [He blasts his victim.] Yeah, now you know not to fuck with Flip-Dogg. You knowhatimsayin'? Ain't that right, Jay? Now they know not to fuck with Flip-Dogg. [He sits.] I'm the baddest motherfuckin' thug-ass dogg, straight up, Jay. Whooh!

Ah. [He takes a breath.] It's good to be back on your show, Jay. Thanks for havin' me on, man. Yeah, you know, I get all the bitches. I got mad gees and shit. Nah, I'm just kiddin'. But yeah. It ain't easy bein' the number one rapper in the world, man. But me and my homies, Montana Gangsta Blood Thugs, we keep it real. Our album is the dopest shit you ever heard. It sold thirty-five million copies. Actually it sold three hundred fifty billion copies. The whole planet bought our record, Jay. .....Yeah, it's tough tourin', bein' on the road. You know, signin' autographs and ridin' around in limousines and drinkin' champagne every day and whatnot. Ten bitches up in my hotel room. Fuck it, I got four hundred seventy-three bitches up in my hotel room. But, it's all good.

[He is interrupted again.] What?! I told you I left it on the counter. .....If it ain't there, Dad musta picked it up. .....Well, Dad musta picked it up then. .....I don't know! Bowling!

. . . Damn. The fans, Jay, they won't leave me alone, man. [He stands in front of the mirror again.] I know what you're thinkin', Jay. You're thinkin', like, "How is it that this white dude could be such a dope rapper?" Well, the truth of the matter, Jay, is that I ain't white, man. I'm really black. See, I went to the doctor, Jay. This is between me and you, Jay. And he told me I got this rare skin disorder where I look white but I'm really black. It's called like eosinophilic ionic . . . dermatitis. Like, check this out, see this birthmark, Jay? Well, it's not really a birthmark, see that's the real color of my skin, and the rest of me is a birthmark. It's mad rare. The shit is mad rare, Jay. But I mean, even though I live in Montana, I still got the ghetto in my heart. I mean, this is just temporary. I'm just chillin' here for now. I don't really belong here. I'ma move soon though. I'ma move to like . . . just to some straight-up ghetto thug-ass projects type shit. Where the people just kick it every day and keep it real. And chill in their BMWs and rap, and all the girls got on bikinis, and everybody just . . . parties . . . and raps. You know, where the niggas just kick it, Jay. Don't get me wrong. When I say "nigger," I don't mean it like in any bad way. Like, "Oh you fuckin' nigger." But like, when you're just chillin' with your homeys and you just be like . . . I don't know . . . "What's goin' on, you bitch-ass nigga!" It's all good. It's all love, Jay. It's all love.

[He is interrupted again.] I don't gotta work till five o'clock! If I don't gotta work till five o'clock, then I don't gotta leave till four-forty, and it ain't four-forty yet. It's four thirty-eight! .....So I'll leave at four-forty then. .....No! He took it back to the feed store yesterday, I don't have it! .....Don't come in my room! I'm naked!

[He sulks over to where imaginary Jay sits.] Damn. Man, see what I gotta deal with every day? Oh, I'm sorry I'm standin' on your fuckin' head, Jay. You little fucker. [He goes back to the mirror.] So, yeah, Jay, I gotta leave soon, man, I gotta work, Jay. .....Hardee's. I mean, I don't need to work at Hardee's, 'cause I'm a millionaire fuckin' rapper. But, you know I like to just help out my community every now and then, you knowhamsayin'?

[Beat] But I hate it sometimes though, Jay. I mean, that ain't me, man. I'm just standin' there, servin' burgers to some damn tractor-drivin' motherfuckers. Bunch of biscuit-head bitches whinin' to me for extra ketchup. Man, fuck that. These people are stupid. You gotta see 'em, Jay. All they do is hang out at the mall every day, and just walk back and forth all day from Foot Locker to Chi-Chi's, Chi-Chi's to Foot Locker. Then they go home and watch *Friends* and *Cops.* Yippee. Those are wack fucking activities, Jay. Are you feelin' me? I don't really aspire to that in my life, man. I want fuckin' . . . I want . . .

I mean, what the hell I wanna be white for? The shit is stupid. . . . Look at you, you're corny, Jay! If I had a choice between bein' like you—Jay Leno—or Tupac Shakur, who you think I'ma choose? . . . Tupac! I mean . . . he's dead. But at least he went out like a true thug nigga. *He's* cool. *You?* You're just a dick, Jay. At least Tupac kept it real. Are you even *in* reality, Jay? You just *sit* there.

[Alas, another interruption] . . . All right, I'm comin'! [Back to Jay] I gotta go help my moms start her truck. I'm sorry for bustin' on you, Jay. It's all love, man. You know you my main nigga. But I'ma be back, man. You watch out. And look out for my new album, *Montana Gangsta Blood Thugs, Ghetto Rollin': Comin' fo' That Ass in the Two Gee.*

[He exchanges his baseball cap for a Hardee's cap, looks at himself for a moment, and then adjusts it into a more favorable position.] Keep it real, Jay. [He exits.]

PAULA COURT

SAM

[A corrections officer in his thirties sits in the waiting room of an upstate New York psychologist.]

HI, HELLO. HOW ARE YOU? .....Who are you? Oh, you're Dr. Lemings? Yeah, hi, hello. Sam Knoll. .....Oh, I thought you were the secretary. .....You don't have a secretary? Oh, that's cheap. I mean, that's smart, save money, I don't wanna get into a whole thing. So you're the doctor? . . . Great. .....No, I mean, women doctors, they exist, I don't wanna, ya know . . . go there. .....Oh, you're not finished? You're still with a patient? Well, I mean . . . I'm *here*! On time. I want you to mark down that I arrived for the session on time, because I went out of my way to be on time. .....No, that's all right. I mean, what am I gonna do? You gotta do what you gotta do, I'll . . . I'll make a phone call. .....No, that's all right. I got my own, thanks.

[She leaves. He pulls out a cellular phone and dials.] .....Hi, it's me. Listen, I'm not gonna be there on time, could you wait till seven? .....Because I got caught up with something. .....*Some*thing. Look. I don't want to get into a whole discussion with you about my personal . . . about ridiculousness. I'm asking a favor, Mindy, that's why I'm calling. .....No, I'm not on a date. I'm not even gonna go there with you. I'm at the doctor, Mindy! Are you happy? I just . . . there was an incident at the facility, and I'm fine.

I'm not hurt. .....What does it matter to *you*? .....Well, either you're gonna wait, or you're not gonna wait. That's *your* decision. Look, put Melanie on. ......You wanna yell at me, Mindy, yell at me in person, don't yell at me on the phone. Okay? How does that sound? That sound good to you? Put Melanie on, please. .....Because she's my daughter, I wanna talk to her!

[Cheery] Hi, Melanie honey, it's Daddy. I miss you so much, sweetie-pie. Tonight's Daddy's night, honey, you remember? Are you excited? I'm excited. Hey, Melanie, you wanna go to White Castle and play video games? Mmm, yummy! .....No? Okay, well we can do anything. Listen, Melanie honey, Daddy's gonna be a little late picking you up, okay? And I have a feeling that Mommy is gonna try and take you with her before I get there. So if Mommy gets angry, you know how Mommy gets upset? You know—[growling]—grrrrr. And she tries to leave? You tell her, "No, Daddy's picking me up." Okay? .....Because Daddy had to go to the doctor, sweetie-pie. .....Because Daddy hit a prisoner. .....No, Daddy's fine. Daddy has no cuts or bruises or scratches or anything. Daddy just has to *talk* with the doctor about what happened. .....No, the prisoner is not fine, honey. But Daddy's fine, that's what counts. Okay? [He waves to the doctor, who has reappeared.] Uh, I gotta go, sweetie-pie. Remember, I'm coming to pick you up. .....No, I don't wanna talk to Mommy again. Don't put Mommy on the phone! Hang up the phone, Melanie. Okay? Just hang up. Bye.

[He hangs up and turns to the doctor.] Heh. My kid. Did you mark down that I came in on time, because I don't want to get penalized because *you* forgot. Because I know how these things work. I mean, I'm sorry if I was, you know, on the phone when you came in, but you weren't exactly . . . *available* for me, either, when *I* arrived on time. Okay, so maybe *I* acted questionably as a corrections officer, and *you* acted questionably as a psychoanalyst, or whatever you call yourself. Hey, that makes two of us. Bingo! We all win a prize. [He folds his arms.]

.....No, we're separated. I'd rather not discuss that with you. .....What *would* I like to discuss? I don't know, you tell me. I mean, I know I'm here because you're supposed to dissect my brain and figure out where my "rage" is coming from because the report says that I "overreacted." Well, I'll tell you right now like I told the board: I did not overreact. I was provoked and my life was threatened and I was forced to strike and contain the inmate. But you got these groups that say, "Oh, the officers are a bunch of animals walking around beating up on the guys for fun—"

Aren't we gonna go in your office? .....You just wanna give your patient some time? .....Time for what? .....Regroup? Regroup what? Oh, that's great, what, is she crying? Oh, that's great. .....It's a *man*? Oh! Bingo. Let's have a party. Listen, I was here on time and I gotta pick up my kids, and I'm not gonna stay longer because some emotionally unprepared fruit fly is weeping to death in your office. It's not gonna happen. I mean, how long is he gonna be? How long does it take to cry?

.....Two. I have two kids. .....Why did we separate? Okay, fine. I know we're supposed to have an open exchange. I'm open. To freely exchange with you. .....You mean, what event actually caused it, or just like . . . why? .....Okay, fine. Well, I'm sittin' there in the pancake diner with her and the kids. Uncle Pancake House. And she's on Prozac first of all. So automatically she starts crying some stupid ridiculous nonsense bullshit. All I said to her was, I don't even remember, like, "I still like you" or something. She's also on her period, okay? No offense, but I mean, you know . . . uh. So, out of nowhere she's like, "Uhhhh ooohh." Crying. I just said, ya know . . . "Oh, that's nice, I'm not gonna get into your shit." You know? "How 'bout those Buffalo Bills?" I think I said. Or something like that.

Aren't we supposed to talk about the incident? I mean, what is this? Some kind of little casual, impromptu, ya know, probe into my shit? I mean, what the fuck is *this*? I'm sorry. I'm not angry at *you*. I'm perfectly happy to be here. You're very nice. I'm very happy. . . . Maybe you should check on your friend back there, maybe he's dead. I'm sorry. I'm just kidding. That's cruel. I'm not a cruel person. I just, I mean, maybe he's finished, that's all. And he's just sitting there. With the tissues.

. . . We're just gonna wait? *I* have patience. I'm a patient man. I'm a patient; I'll be patient. How does that sound? . . . How 'bout I tell you a joke one of the assholes told me—excuse me—one of the *inmates*. It's just something we call 'em. It's just a nickname really. Anyway. Let me try and remember properly. . . . Okay. There's this guy, and he lives somewhere rural. I mean, not unlike around here, but more primitive. So he goes to buy some live chickens, from the live-chicken store. But he doesn't have any money. So he says to the man, "Hey, buddy, I don't have any money, but if I tell you where each of these chickens come from, how 'bout you give me them for free . . . hmm?" So the man says, ya know . . . "What? Who are you? That's impossible. No." Ya know, "Wait a second, what are you talkin' about?" I mean, that's not exactly what he says, but . . . it doesn't even fucking matter, it's just a stupid joke.

So the guy takes his finger, and he sticks it up into the first chicken—'cause there are three chickens; I mean, there are more than three chickens in the whole place, but in the joke there's three that are essential to get to the end—so he sticks his finger in the chicken's . . . ass, and he, ya know . . . and he says, "This chicken is from . . . San Juan, Idaho." There probably isn't even a place San Juan, Idaho. I'm not familiar with maps really. But it doesn't matter really where the chicken is from. But he's *correct,* is the gist. So the owner says, you know, "Wow! Yes, that's right, that chicken *is* from . . . yes. My goodness," ya know. "Wow." Then the guy sticks his finger up in the second chicken, and he says, "This chicken is from, ya know . . . Alaska!" It's probably too cold for chickens there, but again he's, ya know . . . let's just say he's correct. So now, the store owner is more . . . astonished than with the first chicken: "This is amazing. Whoa, you really knocked me off my . . . spaceship there," or whatever the fuck the guy says. Then the guy sticks his finger in the third chicken, he says, "This chicken is from ya know, I don't know . . . Florida." It's unimportant. So, the owner says, "Wow! Take the chickens!" But just then, this bum, this . . . derelict, this . . . unkept person walks by, and sees what's going on, and says to the guy, "Hey buddy, uh, could you stick your finger up in *me*? I'm lost."

. . . It's not funny. But see, this is what I'm subjected to every day is what I'm trying to explain to you. I'm exposed to this kind of . . . ridiculousness and mentality. I mean, I'm not complaining about my job. I like my job. It's just these guys they send up here from downstate, from the city, they're like pollutants. Can you imagine if we let them loose in the middle of town? They'd probably slaughter the cows walking around. I mean, they slaughter *each other*. Not that I mind. Like for instance, last week this one inmate cuts open the face of another inmate. The one guy lost a lot of blood, got transferred downstate, the other inmate got transferred further upstate. Good riddens. Ya know? I still get paid.

But like I said, I can't complain. I got my health insurance, I got my new Isuzu truck. My kids got health insurance. The older one's got braces, all paid for. Of course, I only get to see my kids once a month. Because my wife won't let me. Because we're separated. Because I'm an alcoholic. But you wanna know something? So is she. So what do you think of the justice in *that* court decision? Heh. What do you think of *them* apples?

"What do you think of them apples?" That's funny. You know they say that phrase originated in this county? Oh yeah, this whole town used to be apples. Famous New York State apples. My grandfather had an apple farm. My father had an apple farm. I used to pick apples. But of course, you know, there's only so lucrative you're gonna get with apples. I mean, what are you gonna make? Apple juice, apple sauce. Ya know, apples. I mean, that's . . . heh . . . But when they built the facility, that was the largest economic boom in the history of the county since the thirteen colonies. So, ya know. You gotta go with the boom. If I didn't go with the boom, I'd still be pickin' apples. What kind of life is that? Now we get our apples from Washington. Heh. That makes sense.

Look, I'm not blind, I see where you're tryin' to push this little happy discussion. I know what your job is, okay? It's very helpful talking to you. Yeah. I'll tell ya. I'm not the one you should be talking to. I'm not one of these guys on my shift, calls me up four o'clock in the morning about to drive his truck off one of the goddamn Adirondacks. You wanna counsel somebody? Go counsel *him,* don't fuckin' counsel *me.* Okay? Maybe I drink, but I *sleep*!

Look, I got plans, okay? I did twelve years already with this. I got eight more. Then I'm out. Get my pension. Open a little gift shop. . . . For the women, you know. They come up on the bus from downstate. They bring gifts for their husbands, but they don't realize till they get up here, ninety-five percent of it they can't bring inside: cakes, books, pens. You can't take that stuff in. I'm gonna have a store—all items permissible to enter. Freeze-dried soups, magazines, socks. Put it right by the bus station. Have some financial security.

Listen, can I go pick up my kids? That sound good to you? 'Cause I got one night with them. And you might try and take away my job, but you're not gonna take away my one night with my kids. *That* you're not gonna take. How does that sound? .....Oh. Thank you. Yeah. And I'll see you next week, and I'll be on time—and make sure you marked down I was on time today, because like I said, I know how these things work. Okay. . . . Have a nice evening. [He exits.]

PAULA COURT

GABRIEL

[A young man in a Yankees jacket and hat sits in front of several doctors and rehabilitators in a conference room at Montefiore Medical Center, Bronx, New York. He speaks with a severe speech disorder.]

GOOD AFTERNOON, LADIES AND GENTLEMEN. My name is Gabriel Messenger. I live in the Bronx, New York City. I'm nineteen years old. I go to Bronx Community College. I'm class of 2000. . . . Yay. I study liberal arts. I don't have a major yet. Maybe business. Maybe art. I like . . . paint. Also I like . . . the Yankees. . . . Can you tell?

I also intern, part-time, for the Sanitation Department. . . . I type, fifty, fifty-five words per minute, part-time. For Sanitation Department. As a intern. Maybe, if I'm having a bad day, like if the Yankees lose, I only type forty-five. Or maybe only type forty if they lose the play-offs like they did last year. They're so stupid!

Anyway . . . oh—my cousin takes me to almost all the Yankee games when he don't gotta work. He's cool. But he only get cheap tickets that's really far, 'cause it's only six-fifty. It looks like ants playing baseball. You know . . . ants? . . . Sometimes you don't even know who won. . . . I tell him, "Why you so cheap?" He says, "Shut up, Gabriel." But he's cool. My cousin. He works in a nightclub in Manhattan. The Palladium. Wow. He's a bouncer, I don't know why, 'cause he's so . . . skinny. I told him, "Why they let you be a bouncer . . . you look like Shaggy from *Scooby Doo*?" [He laughs.] He says, "Shut up, Gabriel!" I say, "You shut up!" Then we watch ants playing baseball. And they lose . . . I think.

Um . . . anyway, I know alotta you doctors and nurses know me, seen me around here for last ten years. Maybe some of you new doctors and nurses don't know me. . . . My mother, she smoked cocaine when she was pregnant. That's why my face is a little distorted, and my speech is distorted too. My speech therapist . . . therapist. Her name is Lynn Schlansky. (You try 'n' say that name. You all need speech therapy say *her* name.) She's cool. 'Cause alotta therapists boring, like, they make you read the newspaper—boring. Or books, like Edgar Allan Poe—boring! But she's cool. She lets me bring my rap albums, like KRS-One, the Fugees, Tribe Called Quest, or whoever, and she lets me rap to it, as part of the session. . . . Even all the dirty words. But she makes me say it right. Shh! . . . It don't matter, it's her last day, what you gonna do?

Anyway . . . you not gonna see her around here anymore. And probably not gonna see me around here anymore either. . . . Anyway, we gonna miss her, a lot. So, thank you for everything, Lynn Schlansky.

V. AMESSÉ PHOTOGRAPHY

DANNY'S TRIP TO L.A.

SO I HAD JUST GOTTEN BACK FROM CUBA, where I was invited to perform my show at the International Theatre Festival in Havana and I was the only representative from the United States, and definitely Brooklyn. I had just gotten off the plane in New York, and I get this call from my agents. "It's urgent," they tell me. It's urgent 'cause the people from *Seinfeld* had called them. They wanted me to get on a plane the next morning to guest star in an episode of *Seinfeld*.

Now, I was just hangin' out with these young Cuban students that were really cool and inspirational, and now I'm being asked to hang out with . . . Seinfeld. Who's like . . . the antithesis? I mean, maybe not for you, but you know, I don't know you, you could be whoever. In fact you probably *are* whoever. But I just got off the plane from Cuba, so I'm kinda disoriented, and I start thinkin': I don't really watch *Seinfeld*. But the few times I've seen clips of it, or it was on in somebody's house, I never really had a problem with it. Then these voices start comin' in my head, like, "Do you know how many actors would kill to be in this position?"

So I'm thinking. And I start thinkin' about all the young people I've seen in jail, when I worked in jails—some of them aspiring actors—who used to ask me, "Hey, you're pretty good, why aren't you on TV?" And I thought, "Damn, I don't know!" I mean, I worked hard, I paid dues. I trained to be an actor. Of course, my views on what an actor is had changed after doing theatre in jail for four years, but still.

Then I start to figure, you know . . . everybody loves *Seinfeld.* Even my hardcore roughneck friends, my hardcore political friends, my leftist friends, my Black Panther friends, my Puerto Rican Indepentista friends, even my communist anti-white-male-power-structure friends love *Seinfeld,* so what could go wrong? It seemed like everywhere I turned—everyone I called in that *one hour* I had to decide—everyone seemed to not only have no problem with *Seinfeld,* but they really liked *Seinfeld.*

Then I got all amped. I was like, Nah, wait a second. I'ma be on *Seinfeld!* All these people are gonna see me and be like, "Oh shit, I seen you on *Seinfeld,* ahh . . . ," and that can't feel too bad. So I read through the script, and I'm laughing here and there. It's funny. It's one of these *Seinfeld* episodes that doesn't really have a plot, it's just got *subplots.* . . . You know you watch the shit.

So the main *subplot* is that the guy who takes care of the pool and collects towels at Jerry's health club wants to befriend him. He's really enthusiastic in an almost psychotic way about spending time and hangin' out with Jerry. There are some funny moments. Eventually the guy shows up at Jerry's place wanting to hang out, and Jerry disses him. The guy gets pissed off and ultimately, at the end of the show, puts dirty towels in Jerry's locker. Ha-ha.

There's one thing, though: The character's name—the "Pool Guy" as he was called in the script—his name was *Ramon.* So I'm thinkin', I wonder why his name is

Ramon? I mean, this is 1995, this is *Seinfeld*. I know this can't be the stereotypical Spanish-speaking "Pool Guy," who is psychotic and funny and crazy, and jumping up and down, and that's it. So we call up and we ask. And the casting guy or the producer guy says, "Oh no. No no no no no no no no. Not at all. They saw you on HBO, they love you, you can make him whoever you want." I say, "Are you sure? Whoever?" The guy says, "Definitely—he can be whoever you want him to be, he doesn't even need to be Ramon!"

I get to the airport before the sun rises. They fly me out first-class TWA. I'd never flown first class. In all my traveling around the U.S. and the world, I'd never even flown business class, 'cause theatre doesn't have money for that shit. But this is TV and therefore much more important, so you know it's first class all the way.

I get to L.A. and this blond guy picks me up at the airport (no offense), and takes me *directly* to the studio. And all of the sudden I'm actually sitting around a table with Jerry, Kramer, Elaine, and George and like twenty other people. Costumers, stage managers, makeup people, director, assistant director, producers, writers, executive producers. And we all read through the script, and I do the character as this sort of young, uptight, neurotic Brooklyn kid. Kind of like me, but higher strung. . . . And we finish and everybody around the table claps, and leaves to go do their jobs. And now it's just me, the cast, and the director, and we're gonna walk through every scene in the show, and block it.

So I'm in seven scenes, but the first scene I'm not in. And I'm sitting there watching Kramer, George, and Jerry work out their gags in Jerry's kitchen, but for some reason I start feeling like, I don't want to be here, and I feel really hot, and I start getting nervous. I couldn't tell if it was like regular nervousness—like, Oh, I'm on *Seinfeld*—or that kind of awkward nervousness when you're around too many famous people at once. But I didn't feel good, and I was feeling really hot. So my first scene comes up. I'm supposed to greet Elaine as she's leaving Jerry's apartment and come in and bother Jerry. So I ring Jerry's buzzer, say hi to Elaine, do the scene with Jerry, I bother him, you know . . .

But then Jerry and the director, Andy somebody, start whispering something to each other, and then they come up to me and look at me, and one of them says, "So, why don't you do this now in a Spanish accent?"

Well, I looked down at my tattered, fucked-up sneakers, and that's when I realized why I felt hot. I felt like that when I read the script they faxed me. I felt like that on the plane, riding in "first class." And I felt like this six months before when these other people had asked me to be in Quentin Tarantino's *From Dusk Till Dawn* and I read the script and the script said, quote, "INT. Pussy Palace—They enter a bar filled with dirty greasy Mexican whores," unquote. And my agents asked me how could I say no, because Harvey Keitel, George Clooney, and Quentin Tarantino are in it and "Rob Rodriguez is directing, and he's Hispanic! . . . Isn't he?" Well, I looked at my fucked-up sneakers, and my fucked-up sneakers said, "Always listen to your instinct, kid."

I looked up at Seinfeld and Andy the director and I felt kind of like Irene Cara in *Fame.* But I said, "I'm sorry, I can't do that." So Jerry says, "What? Why not?" And I say, "Look, I don't want to waste your time getting into an argument over why not, obviously you have a successful formula for this show, I don't wanna change it, why don't we look for an alternative? Instead of Ramon, let's make him Israeli and he can be . . . Shimon? Or let's make him Ray, or let's keep it Ramon, but not with a Spanish accent."

And Jerry says, "But I don't get it. Is it derogatory? Is it derogatory? Is it derogatory? Aren't you an actor, isn't that your craft, isn't that what you do, you know . . . little accents?" I said, "Well, I play different characters, but why does the 'Pool Guy' *have* to be in a Spanish accent?" And Jerry said, "Because it's funnier that way. His name is Ramon." . . . See, they didn't want the real thing, they wanted somebody that could do the real thing, but still be one of them.

So I said something like ". . . Uh . . . huh? No, I don't think it's funnier that way. Accents aren't funny. People are funny. Like you. You're funny, Jerry. I think."

This, of course, was *not* the conversation I wanted to get into with a group of Jaded Hollywood Millionaire Stars. But I didn't say this in some ill way. In fact, I said it all very apologetically, because they were really making me feel bad, like I was destroying their life's work over something ridiculous and unimportant, and I really felt sorry. But I said, "Look, if you wanted a funny Spanish accent, you should have gotten a funny Spanish actor, from Spain, 'cause that's where Spanish people are from." . . . It's true.

But then Jerry gets on his cellphone and calls the producer, who comes down and gives me this whole guilt speech, like, "It's a half-hour comedy show, what's the big deal? Why did you get on a plane at five o'clock in the morning and fly all the way across the continent for this?" . . . Uh, I don't know. I thought it would be kinda cool, you know . . . *Seinfeld* or whatever.

Then the guy who plays Kramer comes up to me and says, "Look, just do it. Don't even think you're doing a guy with a Spanish accent. Pretend you're doing a guy who's *doing* a Spanish accent"—I swear to God—"'cause otherwise they're gonna replace you, ya know, and you don't want that." I was like, Uh—yes I do!

So we walk through the rest of the scenes, and I'm doing "Ramon" as some other non–culturally specific character that I'm somewhat comfortable with, although I'm already feeling extremely uncomfortable at this point. But in between the scenes come the jokes. Like Jerry says, "So, Danny, why don't you do the next scene in blackface? . . . Oooh!"

Well, I get to the hotel, and I get a call that Friday's rehearsal has been postponed. Now, they don't work on weekends and they shoot on Monday, so when is it postponed until? That night my agent called me and told me the part was recast and I could get on a plane whenever I felt like it and leave. So I did. I left. And they never paid me. Maybe if they at least paid me . . . I wouldn't be tellin' this story. Whoops.

PAULA COURT

ANDY

[A guy in his forties sweeps in a corridor at the Clinton Correctional Facility in Dannemora, New York. He talks to his work-detail partner.]

FOR FIVE-FIFTY AN HOUR? For five-fifty an hour I'll stay in here! They had me on parole, workin' in a McDonald's for five-fifty an hour. I'm doin' the usual thing, workin', you know. Someone comes up and orders a Big Mac and a large fries and a Coke, or they order a twenty-piece McNuggets and three small fries and four Cokes or shakes or somethin'. Right? But there's these old people. I mean they're not like dyin' or nothin', but they're like fuckin' senior citizens, you know? And they come up to the counter and they order a coffee, right? But the thing is, they're takin' six fuckin' hours to order *one coffee.* And I'm like, Hello? What the fuck is it that you want? It's like, they're standin' there, doin' some detailed thing here in the fuckin' place. Meanwhile, behind them there's seventy-five people that are gonna order a hundred fillets of fishes and ninety-five McRibs and they're gonna take two seconds. But you got these people with their fuckin' coffee!

And they come up to the counter like I'm gonna rob them or somethin'. Hello? I'm a drug addict, not a thief. You know? If I wanted to rob you, would I be standing there behind the counter in my

McDonald's fuckin' costume, asking for your fuckin' order?! Huh? Would I? I'm like, "Just order your coffee, pay your fifty-two cents and leave me alone." But see, they gotta give me this whole fuckin' thing, like they gotta have it a certain way, and they don't want nothin' in it. I tell 'em, "Look, I'm not doin' nothin' to the coffee, it's black, you could have all the creams and sugars you want, and here's *five stirrers.*" But no, because that's not good enough for them either, 'cause they got a heart condition or somethin', like I give a fuckin' shit! I got AIDS, you wanna compete with *me,* you wrinkled fuckin' Sun-Maid raisin motherfuckers?

This one guy comes back three hours later, complainin' about the coffee that he already fuckin' drank, that it tasted like shit, or like piss or whatever. I said, "What the fuck you want me to do, asshole? What?! You want more choices? Go to Starbucks, you fuck! Don't fuckin' bother *me!*" He says, "Oh, you're not treating me like a customer should be treated! What about the rights of the customer? This is America, I'm the customer!" I said, Yeah? Fuck you, customer! Fuck-you-customer! Then he starts complainin' to the manager that *I'm* a fuckin' asshole. Psst, yeah. For five-fifty an hour I'd rather stay right here in jail, thank you very much.

[To another guy] Hey what's up, Mauricio, how you feelin'? You workin' commissary today? .....Don't pick your nose next to the food, huh? Ya fuck.

[Back to the first guy] Plus, at least in here I get medical attention for my fuckin' AIDS. You think *McDonald's* is gonna pay for it? Yeah, Ronald McDonald, "Do-do-di-doo, here's two hundred thousand dollars for your medication, sir, french fries with that?" Yeah, what a fuckin' joke.

.....Huh? Ah, I know, alotta the guys can't tell that I got it. Well fuck, nobody can! I gotta watch out for the TB though. 'Cause these kids they're shippin' up here from Riker's, I heard half of them got it 'cause the ventilation's fucked up down there. And it's no better in here. And me, I got no fuckin' immune system and shit. They're feedin' us this crap in here, it's all starchy shit. It lowers your immune system. We might as well be eatin' at fuckin' McDonald's. .....No, when I was outside, I was eatin' all organic food, everything organic. . . . I was shootin' heroin, but I was eatin' organic. 'Cause the chemicals they spray the food with, and the drugs that they grow it with, it fucks up your immune system, man. It stresses you out too. It keeps you down. It makes you depressed. And the doctor said I can't afford to get depressed. He said I gotta keep a optimistic attitude about life. I think I'm doin' a pretty good job. .....No, I feel really enthusiastic about a lot of shit sometimes. .....What? I don't know really.

Like when they serve carrots in the mess. I fantasize that they're organic, and they're not overcooked and soaked in rancid butter and Percodan. It makes me smile. . . . Or when they show *Gilligan's Island* on TV. Oh, I love that show. The Skipper, that's my motherfuckin' man! I love that motherfucker! .....I don't know, for some reason I relate to like his plight, you know? It's like he's stuck on this island with all these stupid . . . fuckin' nuts. I mean, he's not too bright if ya think about it. Actually, he's a fuckin' dummy. But I don't relate to that part. Like when he suffers, I relate to that. Like this one time, Gilligan finds this shrine of coconuts on the beach that belong to these headhunters. So what does he do, the schmuck he is? He starts kickin' the coconuts all over the fuckin' beach, like soccer. So of course the headhunters get pissed off and tie everybody up and they're gonna burn 'em and kill 'em. So the Skipper's like, "Gilligan, why'd you kick the coconuts?! You stupid schmuck bastard asshole!!!" I mean he didn't say that on the show, but that was his subtext. I relate to his plight, his anger. But ya know, I mean . . . it's just a show.

What I'm sayin' is, I just try to engage myself in shit to stay up. So I don't get bored. Like I like to have meaningful conversations with people. Like with you. You're not stupid. You can carry a conversation. Not like some people, can't complete a sentence, they gotta talk with their hands. You wanna have a conversation with them, you gotta have a fuckin' fight.

You know Sharif? The imam, the guy that runs the Muslim services? That guy can have a conversation. Oh yeah, we debate for hours about shit. He's a friend of mine. He got sent up a week after me. We play chess in lower rec.

Check this out. Like a month ago, me and Sharif are sittin' in the rec. The guys are watchin' TV, and the Martin Lawrence show comes on, and it's everyone's favorite show. So in this episode, Martin is takin' his girl out for a night on the town. So they get all dressed up nice and shit, and they go to this fancy club. So he's at the bar gettin' her a drink. She's at the table, sittin' there, and this guy walks up and starts talkin' to her: "Hey baby, you're lookin' good tonight, whatever whatever. What's your phone number et cetera." But this guy's a clown. His hair is like three times the size of Ronald McDonald and Snuffeluffugus put together, and he's got like juice drippin' off it, like orange juice, or Jheri juice, whatever the fuck he put in it. And he's got about twenty-five gold chains around his neck, with like a dick on it or somethin'.

And he's wearin' a Gucci jumpsuit with Gucci shorts, or like a Gucci ski suit or somethin'. But it's the same guy—it's Martin! They did like a camera trick, you know, the way they filmed it or whatever. So he's boppin' around, "Hey baby, what's the matter, you don't like my style?" he says. Heh-heh.

So everybody's crackin' up except this one kid. This fish. Just got sent up for murder. He can't be more than nineteen years old, the kid. So the kid's sittin' there like this, lookin' at Martin like this . . . all angry and shit. All the sudden, he gets out of his chair, he goes, "Fuck that nigga!" . . . So Sharif tells him he can't use that word. 'Cause, you know, even if you're black, you can't use it, cause the Muslims'll discipline ya. The kid goes, "I don't care, fuck the Muslims, and fuck that nigga Martin Lawrence!" I say to myself, ya know . . . "Uh-oh! Uh-oh!" Then everybody starts lookin' at each other, like . . .

He walks up to the TV screen, and he says, "Can't you see, can't you see? He's darker than he was before!" Like he put makeup on, so he would look darker to play the buffoon guy with the nest on his head and whatever. So now everybody starts lookin' at each other again. Like—you know, all like, whoa . . . eh, confused and shit.

I mean, we're a bunch of locked motherfuckers in jail, one second I'm sittin' with the guys watchin' the Martin Lawrence show, then this kid's about to get fucked up, and then we're like, huh? You can imagine . . . the complexness, it's just this completely rare bugged-out fuckin' situation taking place. Anyway, then the kid starts talkin' about Al Jolson and whoever. He's givin' a history speech, the kid. He says, "Ah, fuck Martin, what's he puttin' black on his face for—he's *already* black and stupid." I said, "Uh-oh! Uh-oh!"

He goes, "It's fucked up for him to be doin' that. . . ." So I try to calm things down, ya know. I said, "Whoa, take it easy. It's fucked up for him to be doin' that? Look at where *he* is, and look where *you* are! He's ridin' around in limousines, gettin' paid millions of dollars a year for whatever the fuck he's doin', and you're locked up, my friend, with your teeth knocked out at nineteen years old and a scar from your earlobe to your fuckin' mouth. It's fucked up for him to be doin' *that*?" The kid goes, "I don't care, fuck that, fuck you, somebody should complain, somebody should write a letter." [Andy looks perplexed.]

So then Sharif says—and this is why I love Sharif, 'cause he's like a fuckin' lawyer sometimes. I mean he's not, he's an inmate, but anyway he says, "*Somebody* should write a letter? You don't like it? *You* write a letter, you little smart-mouth fuck!" So the kid says, "For what? I'm in jail." So Sharif says, "Oh yeah, if you weren't in jail, you'd write a letter? You'd be sittin' on your couch at home, laughin' at Martin all fuckin' night." But see, now he's locked up, the kid, he's got all this time on his hands, he starts thinkin' about shit. He caught some second-degree charge, he'll be out in 2014. You know what I said? I said to him, I said, "Hey, if I was you I'd write a lot of fuckin' letters." Ha! Ha-ha. . . . It was funny, you had to be there.

I mean, everybody was laughin'. But the kid started cryin'. So I felt bad. I pulled him aside, I said, "Look, my friend, you made a mistake. *I* made a mistake, a lot of us made mistakes. But you better not cry in jail, 'cause you're gonna be in here for a long time." I told him, Look, honestly? Maybe if he *was* sittin' at home, he *would* write a letter. Me personally? Martin Lawrence doesn't really piss me off. He makes me wanna shoot up fuckin' heroin, actually. I mean the guy's bouncin' all over the fuckin' screen for a half hour, ya know? Relax, man. Slow down. Whoa!

But get this. Now he can't get enough envelopes, the kid! He comes by my cell askin' if I got extras. He shows me the letters. "Dear Fox, I think Martin Lawrence is fucked up. Ricki Lake, you're full of shit. Peter Jennings, fuck you." I mean, he explains more, but you know, I'm summarizing. But this is the new millennium! What do you want me to tell ya? I mean, me? I'm gonna die in here. But this shit. This kinda shit excites me. It gets me pumped.

Last week I'm lookin' at one of his letters, he asks me, "How come a white guy got AIDS?" I mean, he knows I'm a shooter, but if it's a conspiracy to kill the blacks, and the gays, and all the other undesirables, how come *I* got it? I mean, obviously, I'm not . . . and I'm also not . . . ya know . . . huh, fuck. You know what I told him? It's a calculated loss, that's why. .....No, lemme tell ya. I was a medic in the Army. I saw these guys they'd bring into the tents in Vietnam. A bunch of dead motherfuckers. Anyway, the point is, when you got a war, when you wage a war against a people or a nation or whoever, you always calculate how many losses you're gonna have of your own. It's called a calculated loss. Look it up in any military dictionary. It's just numbers. Like me in here, I'm just one of two and a half million locked-up motherfuckers. So are you. You don't mean nothin'. You're just a number on a fuckin' page. People don't understand that though.

I'm watchin' TV last week, this woman's sittin' in her living room somewhere in the suburbs, moanin', "Oh, my son was killed in Desert Storm, oh, I'm so sad and lonely and whatever . . ." This other one's cryin', "Oh, my husband, now he got chemical warfare syndrome—he can't talk properly, he shits in his pants." You know what? FUCK YOU! Before, you were wavin' your fuckin' flag around all proud patriotic, right?—"Slam Saddam!" and shit. And now you want me to feel *sorry* for *you,* 'cause you're such a victim? I'M SO SORRY FOR YOU, YOU FUCKS! You're a calculated loss! You're a number and that's all you're *gonna* be!

This lady wants money for her son, who's dead? I'm *alive*! There's only so much to go around. But she don't care if I'm on the *street.* Where it's *dirty.* Where maybe I'll shoot up. Maybe I'll shoot *her.* At least in here I *might* get counseling, if they answer my fuckin' requests. I *might* get experimental drugs for my AIDS if they ever read my goddamn letters. No, this lady wants me out there, servin' society, servin' my country. And then one sunny day she strolls into my McDonald's and expects me to just serve *her* and listen to her bullshit, like she *deserves* to be *served*! Lemme tell ya somethin', I SERVED! I served in Vietnam and I served in McDonald's, and I'm servin' sweepin' this fuckin' room all day every fuckin' day sweepin' NOTHIN'! And *I* want SERVICE! I want SERVICES because I'm DYING! *I'M DYING IN THIS MOTHERFUCKER!* [A beat]

[To a guard] Ey, everything's all right over here. Don't push the button, Hal. There's no problem, see, we're just talkin'. Hey, Hal, you don't gotta push the button, see? [He goes back into his monotonous sweeping routine, humming.] Do-do-di-doo. [The guard comes over. Andy hits the floor in a spread position.] Go 'head. Search me. You wanna search me? No problem. I told ya, there's nothin' wrong. No fightin', just got a little excited. See? You don't gotta push the button. [He gets up and continues the sweeping routine.] See? No problem. [Back to his partner] I just got a little depressed there. I told ya, I can't eat the shit they're feedin' us. See, if I eat it, I get depressed, I die. If I don't eat it, I get depressed, I fuckin' die. .....Yeah, it's funny? It's a joke? . . . Keep laughin'. . . . Hey, Mauricio. We got carrots today? .....No? .....Too bad.

V. AMESSÉ PHOTOGRAPHY

VICTOR

[A young man on permanent steel crutches saunters up to a young woman in the waiting lobby of the Albert Einstein College of Medicine, Bronx, New York.]

EXCUSE ME. HELLO. . . . Hello? Hi. What's your name? .....Oh, my name's Victor. Nice to meet you. [Smiling, flirtatious] So, what are you doing here? Oh, wait, lemme guess. You're visiting your grandfather. .....Oh, I was close though, right? She's sick? .....Oh, I'm sorry. You're very pretty, you know that? I mean that you don't seem like the type that you just be chilling in hospitals. You know, I'm not here all the time. I mean, it's not like I be hangin' out here. I just gotta see the doctors for a while like this week and next week 'cause complications . . . well, not really complications, but like . . . somebody had shot me like two years ago, it was a complicated, it was a accident. .....Tsa-ha, don't worry, you didn't shoot me, right?

So, you live around here? .....You sure? I'm saying though, I seen this really pretty girl in 149th Street and I thought it was you, but that wasn't you? .....Oh, a'ight, I'm just makin' sure. You want me to go talk to the guard and see if he could get you in quicker? 'Cause I know him. 'Cause I have to come here every week, not every week, but sometimes, for like rehabilitation, I mean not rehabilitation like I'm a drug addict or some shit like that. But for like, therapy. I mean not like therapy like I'm crazy or some shit like that. But for physical therapy, you know.

.....Nah, I'm not really supposed to talk about it. My mother don't like me to. Not like I do everything my mother tells me, but . . . Nah . . . a'ight. It was two years ago, and I was hanging outside my house, and my friends came by and ask me if I wanna go for a ride, so I got in the car, but I didn't know it was stolen, I mean I had a feeling, but I wasn't sure, I mean you never know, I mean my friend he could have just bought it, but he didn't, but you know, and we drove one block, and the cops stopped us, and they made us get out, and I don't really know what happened. Like, my friend had moved and I guess this one cop thought that my friend had a gun, and he had just . . . panicked or something, I don't know, so he had just started shooting at the car, but I can't really talk about it. They said it was a accident. But I don't know. .....Nah, I mean I was reading in the *New York Post,* and they were talking about like twelve different ways why it could have been a accident. .....No, yeah, I was there but, I mean, I got shot, but the more I read about it, the more I think it might have been a accident.

Damn, you got a nice smile. Where are you from? .....*Staten Island?* Yeah, but I mean you speak Spanish? You're Dominican, right? .....But you're Dominican? .....*Czechoslovakia?* [Smiling] Damn. I'm kinda off, right?! Czechoslovakia, that's near Germany, right? .....Oh, but it's close though, right? I know that 'cause I look at maps a lot. I got maps all over my walls, like in my room. I put them up. I don't know why, I'm just into it. I just like to look at like different places or whatever. . . . So, what they eat over there, like . . . cheese? .....Oh, you never been there? Oh, my bad . . . So, you go to school? .....Ah, see, I could tell, 'cause you got that look. I'm not saying you look stupid, like a nerd. I'm saying you look smart. Like you definitely got plans for your future, like you're on a mission. That's good. What you study? .....Oh yeah? That's good. We need more businesspeople.

Me personally, I would like to go into the Air Force, I mean if they let me, I heard it's still possible. [He glances down at his legs.] .....No, 'cause I would like to protect this country from like evil dictators. Like Saddam Hussein and Fidel Castro. .....Yeah, 'cause like people don't realize that this is the greatest country in the world, you know? .....Yeah, 'cause like, you never know, in other places people could just be savages or whatever, or the government will just shoot you 'cause they don't like you. At least here we got democracy, and everybody's protected. .....Right, right. But mostly, I would like to be able to fly like a F-15, or a Stealth bomber, 'cause then I would get to just fly over all those places in the maps. .....Nah, I wouldn't stop nowhere. I would just fly over, you know, look at it . . . maybe drop a few bombs or whatever.

So, you watch TV? You like *Seinfeld*? .....Oh, that's my favorite show. .....Yup. Last week, they had this Mexican guy in it. He wasn't Mexican, but he was playing like he was Mexican, but it was funny. . . . Damn, they make you wait a long time out here, right, just to visit somebody. You sure you don't want me to ask the guard, and see if he could let you go upstairs? .....You sure? .....Oh, a'ight. I'm just making sure. .....Right. . . . So . . . would you like to go out with me sometime? I mean, I ain't Tom Cruise or nothing, but I'm Puerto Rican. You know what they say about Puerto Ricans, right? We're good dancers. For real. You didn't watch in the Discovery Channel Entertainment Report? .....They discovered us. They did a whole thing that said Puerto Ricans are the best dancers in the world. I mean, they didn't say it, but that's what they were saying, you know. I bet you like to go dancing, right? You like to go to clubs in Manhattan? .....What music you like? I could dance to anything—house, hip-hop, salsa, merengue, classical, whatever.

You don't think I could dance, right? I could dance. I been practicing for the past two years. Besides, they said in the Discovery Channel that it doesn't matter, as long as you're Puerto Rican. You and me could dance right here, to practice. It's nobody looking. ......It's nobody looking though. [She walks away.] .....Oh, a'ight, nah, that's a'ight, I understand. Yeah. ......A'ight, well, tell her I hope she feels better, all right? . . . Good-bye. . . . It's nice meeting you. . . . It's the fourth floor. . . . Push the button. . . . You're very pretty.

PAULA COURT

PETER

[A young student is selling clave sticks and other crafts in the Marqueta de Artesanía in La Habana Vieja, Cuba. He works the street with a friend, playing the sticks and yelling to the Italian, German, French, and Swiss tourists, trying to get their attention.]

UNA CLAVE AUTÉNTICA CUBANA POR AQUÍ por un dólar! ¿Quién la quiere? ¡Yo tengo la clave más Cubana que todas! ¡Hecha de madera dura, durísima de Pinar! Yo tengo los buenos precios, los mejores precios en La Habana entera!

[He follows one man for a few steps.] ¡Mira, señor! ¿Tú no quiere comprar una clave por un dólar? Espérate un momentico, yo no te voy a dañar. Esta es madera dura y auténtica. De Pinar del Río. . . .

[He follows a woman.] ¿Señora, usted no quiere una clavecita preciosa por aquí? Un dólar. . . . Pa' que usted la lleve pa' tu país o dondequiera. Llévate una. . . . ¿De dónde tú eres? ¿Italiana? ¿Italiana? ¡Ciao, que bella! . . .

[He follows another man.] ¿Qué volá, mi asere? Una clave presquecita por un dólar, compay. ¿Usted no la quiere? Chacho, pero . . . [He takes a break and sits, deflated. It's not a good day. To his friend] Felito! Es que no hay ni un cliente hoy. ¿Qué lo es que vamos hacer, brother?

[Another tourist appears. Peter blocks his path.] ¿Mira, señor, tú no quiere comprar una clave auténtica Cubana? Esta es, de madera durísima de una mata . . . grandota y vieja, con hojas que te pueden cubrir. Un dólar. Mira como suena. [He demonstrates.] .....No, pero espérate un momentico, no te quiero dañar ni nada de eso. Yo no estoy aquí jineteando ni nada de eso. Esto es mi negocio. ¿De dónde tú eres? ¿Italiano? ¡Ciao! ¡Que bello! .....¿No? ¿Francés? ¿Tú eres Francés? ¡Bonjour! ¡Bonjour! ¿Cómo talle vou—oui oui oui oui oui? ¿ .....No? ¿España? Thincuenta y thinco thentavoth-th-th-th! No? United State? .....United State? ¡Ah! You live in United State? Pero espérate un momentico por ahí, asere. No te vayas pa' ningún lado, yo no te voy a dañar, coño.

¿Este . . . you live United State? You speak some Spanish? .....No? Pero . . . you live in United State! ¿No? No te preocupes. Is okay. I speak some English. I learn, allí mismo, en la University of La Habana. I am engineer estudent. Engineer . . . Ingeniero soy. Is you first time here en Cuba? .....You like? ¿Mira, you don't want buy one clave por un dólar? .....Un dólar. Okay.

Bueno mira, venga acá, este. . . . Where you live in United States? [He mimes it.] WHERE—YOU—LIVE—IN—UNITED—STATES? .....New York? New York City? ¡Nueva York! Chacho, claro pués . . . [He shoots imaginary guns in the air.] You live close Michael Jackson house? .....No? You live close Michael Jordan? .....Michael Jordan. .....Pero you know who is Michael Jordan. [He turns to his friend for a second.] ¡Felito, cállate tú la boca por un minuto! ¡Este tipo es amigo de Michael Jordan, coño! [He turns back.] No le haga caso ninguno.

Este . . . mira . . . What music you listen en United State, en New York? You listen the Cuban salsa? . . . La

Charanga Habanera, Los Van Van, Paulito y Su Élite, quien sea. .....¿No? ¿Ni la moña? You listen la moña? .....¡La moña, compay! La música rap. Este . . . Esnoo Doggy Dogg, Biggie Esmall . . . Wu-Tang Clan, Doctor Dre, Ice Cube, Ice-T, Brand Nubian, este . . . Too Short . . . Too Short . . . este—Demasiado Bajito por ahí—Too Short. Aha. . . . Quién más, este . . . Tupac Shakur—¡*Tupac Shakur*, compay! Tupac Shakur! Venga acá. ¡Yo soy fanático de Tupac! ¡Tupac Shakur es, para mi . . . como un Dios!

Mira, yo soy rappero. I am . . . rap. Felito también, Él es mi homie. Nosotros somos homies ya, desde hace muchos años. Felito y yo, we have one group of rap—Los Rapperos Crazy Wow. Y ya hace tres meses . . . ¿como se lo dice?—Rappeamos, en el festival, de música, allí en Alamar. . . . Oye—"¡Yo soy Cubano, pa' que tú lo sépa, cuando rappeo en micrófono, to' el mundo dice—huépa!" You like? .....You no understand any word I say? Bueno, imagínate, bro, you livee United State.

You know one song call *"Apenejé"*? .....¡"Apenejé," "Apenejé"! .....Sí, from United State! ¡From New York viene! Va . . . "Apenejé, Hop, Hibbi, Hibbi tu la Hi-Hi Hobby, You no stop, check it out bang, bang boogie . . ."—¡"Apenejé," bro! Man, mi homie, esa canción, completamente—me cambió la vida!

¿Y venga acá yo, you no breakea? .....Breakea, breakea. .....Ah, break-dance, break-dance. Sí sí sí, I am engineer estudent, pero yo hago un tremendo breakeo, bro. Yo andaba breakeando desde niño, compay. Mira, mi homie, yo—gané el concurso Casa de Cultura, La Habana Vieja 93. Mira . . . [He demonstrates.] You like?

Mira, venga acá, man. Peep this, peep this, no? Peep this, man. Una preguntica ahí. Esnoo Doggy Dogg, Esnoo

Doggy Dogg, no? He say one . . . song, una línea, este, one line, from one song, from him, y yo no sé que lo es que significa. Oye, Esnoo Doggy Dogg, he say, "Bitches ain't shit but ho's and tricks, lick on these nuts and suck the dick." Yo, bro man! Chacho, a mi me *encanta* esa línea brother! Esa línea está—arriba de la bola, compay. Man, yo! Pero . . . whas the meaning? .....Ah, you know some word, pero every word you no don't understand, ah, pués ya tú lo sabe. Y también, este . . . Too Short. ¿Te acuerda, Too Short? El rappero más bajito . . . Too Short dice, he say, en el principio from one song, he . . . begin, este, "Hey motherfucker . . . !" Algo así. Pero, porque I study English en university, I know some word, por ejemplo, "Mother" es "Mami." No? Y "fucker" es—por ejemplo, I see some movie from United State, y the people cuando se pone, bien . . . tú sabe—bravo . . . Al Pacino—he say, "Fucker!" O "Fuck you!" O "fucky," o lo que sea. No importa, pero tú me entiendes. Pero, "motherfucker," que lo es que significa, compay? Porque, imagínate, eso no puede ser, "Mami!—Fucker!" Eso no es . . . así. .....Ah, es *idiomático*. Idiomático, claro. Y "hey"? Porque Too Short dice, "Hey, motherfucker . . . " Y "hey" . . . I looking en el diccionario, y "hey" es una cosa—¿verdad, Felito? ¿Una cosa que le dan a los caballos, no?—a comer. "Hey" . . . [He mimes a horse eating hay.] .....Ah, es idiomático también . . . claro.

Bueno y, you no . . . rap? .....No? Pero, you live en New York City. Mira, venga acá. What you do, now? Maybe you come my house, for eat something? .....¿No? .....¡Sí! Sin pena, sin pena! ¡Tú eres mi homie ya! Somos homies. No es problem. You house my house. I am Cuban! I see you here, from the street, you come my house for eat something. . . . Igual que United State—you see some person, from the street, you take you house for eat something, no? [He shrugs.] .....¿Pero qué pasa? .....Ah, imagínate tú. .....Ah. Bueno, pues, no te vayas. ¡No te vayas, mi homie! [The man leaves.] Okay, este . . . ¡See you later, my friend! . . . ¡¿Wasup?!

Felito, venga acá. ¿Viste este tipo? He laughing my English, pero I laughing his country.

PAULA COURT

EMCEE ENUFF

[A famous and very successful rapper in a baseball cap, gold teeth, and Versace shades makes his first appearance on the David Letterman show. He enters in an explosion of flashing lights and loud music.]

EMCEE ENUFF IS IN THE HOUSE! A'ight! Can I get a "a'ight"? .....A'ight! That's my fans out there! Oh, I like that welcome. Yeah. [He crosses to sit with Dave.] It's good to be on your show, Dave. Yeah. Thanks for havin' me on. Oh. Wow. Yeah, man.

.....That's right, that's correct, Dave. My new album will be in stores November twenty-third. It's called *MC Enuff: Where Is the Joy* on Murder-U Records, look out for it. .....Oh, this will be my fourteenth album, actually, Dave. .....Yeah, it's very different from my last album. Actually it's different from all my albums. No doubt. I mean, you talkin' hip-hop is almost twenty-five years old, and there have been many phases, Dave. And me, in my career . . . you know, I've grown and changed and gone through different stages, and matured. . . . Like a fine wine.

.....Well, for instance, you know, I ain't really rappin' about the same stuff I used to be rappin' about in like . . . 1984 or '87 or '93. .....Yeah, well back in '84, I might have said like— .....Oh, don't make me do it, Dave. Don't make me do it! .....Nah, don't make me do it. .....A'ight, I'ma do it, I'ma do it, I'ma do it. Like 1984, I might have said like—oh, a'ight, y'all remember this one:

I'm known in forty nations all over the earth
I been rhymin' every day ever since my birth
I make the girls bring the digits with the flavors I bring
I took your mother on a date we went to Burger King
It's like that, y'all . . .

.....Thank you. Thank you. Yeah. It was sweet. I was young, you know. We used to just chill in the park, make up rhymes. It was just about expressin' yourself, havin' fun. You know, just makin' rhymes about how great I am, or I'm better than you, or I'm the best, or you suck. Little jokes like . . . Burger King or whatever. But now you got:

. . . I got my Uzi, Tec Nine and my AK-47
You get yo dome knocked the fuck off when you come up in my section . . .

.....Basically. .....Oh, the whole East Coast/West Coast conflict? Yeah, I can't really speak about that. .....Nah, I don't really wanna discuss that. I ain't gonna talk about. .....Nah. It ain't . . . Well, no. Fuck it, I'ma talk about it, I'ma talk about it. Yeah, you know, Tupac is dead and Biggie is dead, whatever. And that's negative. But the way I see it, it's about people recognizin' and respectin' each other's cultures. See, the East and the West coasts are two completely different cultures, Dave. Same with Miami, Dallas, Chicago, wherever. We might as well be different nations. I mean, we one nation, but we got different cultures. For instance, you go out to the West Coast, people live in *houses*, Dave. They got room, all spread out, they got space. People on the West Coast be in they house all day like this . . . [He lies back to illustrate.] People drive cars on the West Coast! Big cars, with space in 'em. So their lifestyle is more laid back and . . . spread out. That's why the rhyme style is more laid back. You know, like you bouncin' in your house or car. Like, "I'm just dippin' in my ride, chillin' in the trey," or, "I'm just ridin' round the hood, lookin' for this girl," or, "The sun shines all day," or, "I got so much space around me, I don't even know what to do . . . I might have a barbecue . . ." Or whatever. I mean, that's stupid, Dave, I'm just makin' shit up.

But on the East Coast, we live in buildings, Dave. We live all on top of each other. We walk. I was out there in L.A. recording my tenth album, I tried to walk down the street, get a soda, I was the only one walkin'. Everybody lookin' at me from they cars like, "The fuck *he* doin'?" In New York, we take the subway. We're all squooshed up and mushed against each other. Therefore our lifestyle is just more . . . squooshed. Therefore our rhyme style is gonna be, you know, more squooshed too . . . [He demonstrates.] Like . . . like some . . . Get-off-me type shit. Like . . .

Yeah, motherfucker, call me the rap god
It's the ill kid from Brooklyn with the dick that's
  mad hard
It's the multilinguistic, twisted, the misfit
Bringin' you the sick ballistic freshly dipped shit

.....Thank you. Thank you. But you see what I'm sayin'? You just gotta be true to your lifestyle. I mean, if you come from a place where you got space around you, don't pretend and act like you squooshed up. Or if you come from squooshed, don't front and represent like you spaced out. Just be who you are. If you from Kansas, you know, represent . . . wheat or whatever. I got respect for that. Be yourself. Wherever you from.

It's when people don't recognize and they *dis*respect each other that you got problems. Like for example, let's say you're from Palestine, Dave, and you eat hummus. A'ight? Let's just say. Let's say I'm from Italy and I eat spaghetti. Right? So we sittin' here just kickin' it, right? All the sudden . . . boom—I don't *recognize* your hummus, Dave. You know? I never *seen* your hummus before. Matter fact, your hummus is . . . it scares me. So what do I do? I start thinkin' ill thoughts. Like, Damn this guy, he could do anything with this hummus. He could just . . . you know . . . anything. Wild shit, maybe. So I get up and I kill you.

I mean, not really. That's foolish, obviously. That's not somethin' *I* would do personally, but people out there in the world are ignorant, Dave. What can you do? Let me get back to my point of what I was sayin', which was: As the times change the rhymes change, Dave. Like if you look at the title track off my 1989 album, for example:

It's 1989, you better stay off the crack
All you crackheads stop yo' frontin' in the back . . .

Or:

It's 1992, put down your AK
Have a nice day . . .

'Cause in 1992, guns was everywhere, Dave. By 1989, crack had already infested our communities. Not *your* communities, Dave. But you know what I'm sayin'. And I had to respond to it. I mean, you see these type of things goin' on where you live, you get angry, Dave. I had to do something. I felt like it was up to *me,* Emcee Enuff, to deal with those issues. You know. I started rappin' about, "Stay off the crack, stay in school, don't do drugs, organize, et cetera."

But to be honest, Dave . . . that shit wasn't sellin'. And I had to pay the rent, man. I had house payments. I had people in my studio on salary. I mean, what? I'm supposed to just fire fifteen people? That's un-American. Come on. . . . And plus— .....Yeah, Dave, you know how it is. People don't wanna listen to "Stay in school, don't do drugs, rebuild your community." People want nonsense. People want caca-doodoo-bullshit. That's why you do so well, Dave. No offense, no offense. I mean, you do your thing, I do my thing.

But times changed so *quick.* And you're only as good as your last LP, I had to keep up. And I'll admit it, Dave. I just went through this . . . ill era. You look at my later albums, like '93, '94:

> I want all the pussy, I want all the honeys
> Gimme your car, your wife, your jewelry, and
>   your money . . .

.....Precisely. That's it, I had shifted in my art. I had *shifted.* I just started rappin' about big-booty bitches and runnin' up in niggas' cribs and puttin' fifty bullets in they head, and I got graphic. You know, slicin' somebody's face open, and breakin' open bitches' pussies with my foot, and stuff like that. I did this video, where by the end of the video, I had murdered like . . . seven hundred fifty people. I mean, it was fake, you know.

But actually, I can't even front. Those records made me more money than I ever made in my life, Dave. And I'm grateful to all the French people and the Japanese people, Italians, Swedish people that *bought* those records. All my people in Wyoming, Minnesota, Indonesia, Iowa, Utah . . . Vermont *represent*!

.....Yeah, I *do* feel like I have a responsibility. I mean, let's face it. Everybody knows my name, Dave. I'm a role model. That's why I try to go back to my community—well, what used to be my community. And I just kick it with the young people. I try to tell 'em, "Stay off the drugs! And you must go to college!" That's what I tell 'em. . . . Actually I can't lie—I never went to college and I'm a millionaire, but still—it's important, it's important. . . . Actually I ain't gonna front, I made most of my money when I was *on* drugs, but I don't do it anymore. But what I tell the kids is, "Don't be like me—do not be like me." I mean, I tell 'em, "If you wanna be like me, then . . ."—actually I don't really know what the hell I tell 'em, Dave. I mostly just sign autographs.

I mean, look, I ain't perfect, Dave. I got faults, and so do you . . . that's obvious. But this is what I'm tryin' to say: If you take all my fans all over the world and put them together in one room, tell 'em Emcee Enuff is runnin' for president, they would *vote* for me! That's power! Man, I just did a tour in Japan, I'm standin' there in front of fifty thousand Japanese kids. I started singin' "Murder Every Day," right? They were singin' it *with* me! On some karaoke-type shit. They knew every word to that song. *Every word!* They was break-dancin' out there and everything. I said, This is some *power*ful shit. 'Cause last time I seen breakin' in *this* country . . . was in a Hershey's commercial. That's our culture man, Hip-Hop is alive!

I seen all that goin' on in *Japan,* I had an awakening, Dave. It was ill too. Every night, I would hear my rhymes over and over in my head. Particularly this one line, "Break a bitch pussy, bust a nigga brain/Break a bitch pussy, bust a nigga brain." . . . Say it with me, Dave, "Break a bitch pussy, bust a nigga brain . . ." It just kept repeating itself . . . in my dreams. I got sick. And one morning I just woke up shakin' in a cold sweat, all fucked up and depressed, and . . . rich. And I got out of bed and I looked at myself in the mirror and I just said, "Where is the joy . . . Emcee Enuff?" You know? I'm a millionaire, why is my life filled with such . . . pain, Dave? I ain't gonna front, you got rappers that led ill lives or whatnot. They been to jail or whatever. But see, now they *outta* jail and they rappin' 'bout how great it is and everybody should go. And then 'cause they sayin' that, you got rappers that's *never* been to jail rappin' 'bout how they can't wait to get up in one. That's pain, Dave.

But lemme tell you, and you know this is true, Dave. Once you tasted a fresh tuna sashimi melt in your mouth, you don't wanna go to jail. Right, Dave? . . . You see your mutual fund gain twenty points a year, you be like, "Damn, I'm straight, I don't wanna go to jail." You walkin' down the hot white sands of Barbados or Jamaica or wherever on vacation, you got a fine woman's hand in yours. You go snorkelin' down there, and see all the little stuff on the bottom of the ocean, you like, "Damn—I didn't know this shit was here. . . . Wasup fish?" You like, "A'ight, yeah. . . . *Here* is the joy."

But come on, Dave. If I'm lookin' at bricks and asphalt every day. If I'm eatin' at Burger King for breakfast, lunch, and dinner, and I go to Wendy's for a variety. People ain't givin' me a job, ain't givin' me a loan, ain't givin' me credit. I see somebody who look just like me, gettin' a plunger stuck up they rectum by somebody that's supposed to protect us. Then I *wanna* go to jail. I be like, "Joy? What's that?"

.....Are you following *anything* I just said, Dave? I mean, this isn't just blah-blah-blah, I'm sharing my life here. . . . Thank you. .....Oh, we outta time? Well, thanks for having me on, Dave. . . . I always wanted to be on your show. You ain't ever invite me though. I mean . . . you had squirrels jumpin' through hoops on your show, Dave. I got *fourteen* albums, man. . . . It's easier for a *rodent* to get up on your show, than for *Emcee Enuff* to get on your show. That's what you sayin'. But that's all right though, I don't even care, 'cause you do *your* thing, and I'll do *my* thing.

I'm seein' things in a whole new light now. I feel enlightened, and reenergized and optimistic. I feel type lovely. I feel powerful, Dave. Matter fact, I *am* powerful. I feel like . . . we're gonna change the world—not *you,* Dave, but you know . . . *us.* That's why my new album, *Where Is the Joy,* is on some new improved, extra-ill, enlightened, epiphany-type shit, and that's all I got to say.

.....Oh, don't make me do it, Dave, don't make me do it. .....Nah, I can't, it ain't released yet. Nah, nah, nah, nah. .....A'ight, I'ma do it, I'ma do it. It go like this . . .

Mister Big Poppa, flashin' a hun'ed dolla
Poppin' Cristal at the club, doin' the cha-cha

Actin' drunk, talkin' to mama, sayin' la la
Where is the joy? That shit is caca, da-da

.....Nah, wait. I ain't even finished . . .

I know I got the flavor that the whole world want
But I was wastin' my time, profilin' with my
flaunt
The devil never sleeps and never take no vacation
So now I'm spittin' liberation, not no Gucci
demonstration

People steady mock it, and Congress tries to
stop it,
Cops try to lock it, and Hollywood *co-opts* it
So if we hot shit on the radio station
How come we ain't shit, runnin' this fuckin'
nation?

.....Dave! A'ight? I'm out. No doubt. Peace out.
[He plays to the crowd as he exits.]

SOME
PEOPLE
OCTOBER
18-
NOVEMBER
13
WRITTEN AND PERFORMED
BY DANNY HOCH
DIRECTED
BY JO BONNEY
THE
PUBLIC
THEATER

The only set to this show is a black wooden cube about knee-high, a black stool, and a black chair. These three are moved around in different configurations for each character.

Upstage hangs a clothesline from which the minimal costume pieces hang by clothespins.

An open cardboard box for used costumes sits under the clothesline. The costumes are merely accessories to constant black jeans, T-shirt, and shoes. A hat, a sweater, a blazer, or headphones are grabbed from the clothesline and tossed on quickly for each character change.

WILL HART

CARIBBEAN TIGER

[The scene is a dimly lit radio studio at around one in the morning. The callers, Daddy Sluggy, Clyde, and Sheila, are prerecorded.]

MMM! YES LADIES AND GENTLEMEN of the Big Apple, this is Vaughn Morris your host. Better known to all my fans out there as the Caribbean Tiger! Some people say, what's a tiger doin' in the Caribbean? People well I tell you, livin' up ya inna New York City is like a jungle sometimes and anything can happen, just like a tiger walkin' by upon your radio waves.

Who is listenin' to me? Who is stayin' up with me this early morning, Friday morning, a few minutes after one o'clock people I'd like to know. Call me call me call me. The phone number is 718-555-2828, that's 718-555-2828. The temperature outside right now the weatherman says! About twenty-seven degrees ice cold, people. I tellin' ya, ya better bundle up and stay warm, it's cold outside but never if you're riding with me here upon the radio waves Caribbean Tiger style! Like the man says, you're riding with the Tiger you know it gotta be hot!

Mmm, yes people I'm comin' mixin' up your reggae, rockers, soca, and calypso, oldies but goodies. This hour strictly soca music! We goin' see if you can wind your waist one time. I am lookin' at my telephone switchboard now, my phone lines is blinkin' people! Wildfire inna studio! Worries and Trouble! I'm going to the phones right now. . . . Hello good morning you're on the air . . .

DADDY SLUGGY: Ere dat boss. Wha'appnin', Mister Morris?

Who am I talkin' with this morning?

DADDY SLUGGY: Disya Daddy Sluggy, seen.

Daddy Sluggy! Okay Daddy Sluggy, where you callin' from?

DADDY SLUGGY: Me inna Brooklyn, yeh.

Okay Daddy Sluggy from Brooklyn, you ever call before?

DADDY SLUGGY: Na boss. Aeda check you show fe years, but si is a first time me a pick up de phone an' call you pon radio station, seen.

All right Daddy Sluggy, you want to send some greetings out there?

DADDY SLUGGY: Yeah boss. Ya know first I wan say big up to Pudgy, Mikey, Tinga, and Gary over there in East Flatbush Love Productions. Special request to Big Timer crew,

Sleepy, and all Jamaican people dem, beca ya know seh Jamaica people dem ago run tings inna New York City.

Okay, respect to you, brother.

DADDY SLUGGY: Yeah and greetin's comin' from Daddy Sluggy.

Okay Daddy Sluggy, you have a good night now. You're riding with the most dangerous DJ on the radio, I am the Caribbean Tiger. Raaarr! Watchout Baby! Hello good morning you're on the air . . .

CLYDE: Eh . . .

Hello good morning.

CLYDE: Yes.

Yes, hello.

CLYDE: Yes. . . . Hello?

Yes good morning sir.

CLYDE: Am I on de radio?

Yes you on the radio, would you like to send some greetings out there?

CLYDE: Oh. Yeah. I want to say hello to Roberta, who just arrive yesterday from Port of Spain.

And this is comin' from?

CLYDE: Excuse me?

Wha is you name sir?

CLYDE: Oh. Clyde.

Okay Clyde, where are you callin' me from Clyde?

CLYDE: . . . Yeah.

Yeah, where are you callin' me from?

CLYDE: Huh?

Where are you? Where are you Clyde?

CLYDE: Brooklyn.

Okay Clyde from Brooklyn, thanks for callin' in all right?

CLYDE: Okay, bye-bye.

Okay yes people, the Caribbean Tiger is in the house tonight! Good mornin' you're on the air.

SHEILA: Good morning, Caribbean Tiger.

Whoa ho ho! The Caribbean Tiger is most definitely in the place tonight! Who is this?

SHEILA: This is Sheila. How are you, Mister Morris?

Fine sweetheart, how are you?

SHEILA: Is this a tape? Or am I really on the radio?

Fine sweetheart, how are you?

SHEILA: No, seriously, is this real?

Hello, good morning?

SHEILA: Is this you, Mr. Morris?

Fine sweetheart, how are you?

SHEILA: Stop it, that's no fair.

Ha! Ha! Ha! I'm just playin' with you Sheila. You really tink I'm a tape? Lemme tell you somethin' Sheila, I am live, no jive, never contrive, and I play all you disco forty-five. Raaarr! Where are you callin me from Sheila?

SHEILA: Brooklyn.

Sheila from Brooklyn, are you married?

SHEILA: No.

Do you have a boyfriend?

SHEILA: Yes.

Do you think your boyfriend would mind if I ask you on a date? Because you sound like the prettiest, most beautifulest lady that has called the station tonight.

SHEILA: Maybe not, you have to ask him.

Wha is you boyfriend's name?

SHEILA: Sorrel.

Sorry? Your boyfriend's name is Sorry?

SHEILA: No, Sorrel, like the drink, Sorrel. It's a nickname.

De man name Sorry? What is a pretty lady like you doing with a man call Sorry?

SHEILA: No, Sorrel, Sorrel.

I tell you Sheila dear, I am so sorry about that.

SHEILA: Sorrel!

Do you mind if I ask you on a date?

SHEILA: You tryin' to get me in trouble, Mister Morris?

I don't wanna get you in trouble I just wanna get you telephone number. Ha! Ha! Ha! Tiger-Style Baby, Worries and Trouble! Send some greetin's out there for me, Sheila.

SHEILA: Can you play that Johnny King song for me?

Johnny King! Soca Business! Sheila dear, are you Bajian?

SHEILA: No sir, Guyana.

Guyanese Massive! I'll see if I can't find some Johnny King for you. Thanks for callin' in, Sheila from Brooklyn!

SHEILA: Okay, bye. Love you, Sorrel!

Yes people, the man says lookout, lookout, lookout! Calling all Trinidadian Massive! All Tobagonian! All Bajian, all St. Vincent, all St. Lucian, all Grenadian, all Antiguan, all Guyanese, all Caribbean Massive! The man says this night! Tonight! Friday night! Soca meets calypso over there at the Golden Pavilion over there on Empire Boulevard in Brooklyn, the man says it gonna be HOT! Admission is only ten smackers in this budget deficit time. Security Fort Knox style. The man says is gonna be better than cook food!

And speakin' of cook food people. The records played for you in this fifteen-minute segment is brought to you by Angie's West Indian Restaurant and Bakery over there at 2815 Church Avenue between Nostrand and Rogers avenues and that's in Fun City Brooklyn. Servin up the freshest and most superb in West Indian delicacies. We're talkin about escoviched fish, cow-foot soup, all roti done up just like your grandmother cook it fresh! Tell them you heard it from me the Caribbean Tiger and you get free beef patty. Mmm! Vaughn Morris comes rough every time. Vaughn Morris Is a First-Class Tiger.

PAULA COURT

MADMAN

[It's three in the morning at a Jamaican dancehall spot in the Bronx. One of the live acts for the night, Madman, sporting a leather calabash and sunglasses, pops out of the dark into a spotlight and charms the stage with his romantic ragamuffin stylee.]

YES! A . . . A . . . AHH! LOVE YOU. I want to welcome all de people to de number one night spot inna Bronx. Act Three In The Tropics place. Yes. Fresh and Hot. I want to introduce myself to de people dem. Me a de Madman. Dem a call me Madman beca me mad inna me head, but seh me na crazy. Fresh and Hot! Me a de number one dancehall entertainer fe de people dem. I want to big up all de people who come all the way to check me out tonight. Big up to the Bronx people dem. People from de Brooklyn, de Queens, de Manhattan. New Jersey, go home! Staten Island, stay away! Yes! How many people dem out dere make alotta money? Wole up yu han you make money! Come wid it selector. . . . Me bal—me make de money, ya know me make de money. . . . Cease selector! Fresh and Hot! Me a de Madman. Me na ramp, me na joke, me na skin teeth! Me always come 100 percent Gold Ring, Gold Chain, Gold Tooth, Bally Shoe! And whe eva me go, you know seh me haffe mek a ton a cash. Donald Trump celebrity cyaant touch me bwoy! I love you! I blow a kiss to you! Hug an kiss to each and every person. Special big big super hug an kiss to de gyal wid de fat an healthy body. Me say me love de fat-body gyal. Me na wan no skinny gyal, ca de toothpick gyal mussee garbage pan way. Wole up yu han you don hav a Slim Fast Diet now! Huh! Me a de numba one! I want all my fans to reach out and touch me tonight, because I goin be fresh and hot, like magic inna dancehall place. Touch me, you can touch me, touch me. .....You cyaant touch me. I am too hot. Me a de hot potato. Yes selector, beca you know seh from me born outta me moda belly, me know me is fresh and hot every time. How many people dem out dere you can keep a riddim? How many white people dem can keep a riddim? Not a one, not a one. . . . You can keep a riddim? Follow me . . .

[Audience participation] All first-row people. All second-row people. All third-row people. Fresh. This is a participatory performance process. We ago do this fe about three hours now. Follow me . . .

Me a de Madman, me deh from New York City
Me nah ramp, me na joke, me na skin teeth, people
  don tes me
Me hav de style an de class an de personality
Me seh me walk pon street, people admire me
Alla de pretty gyal dem rush me inna hurry
Dem wan fe me cash an fe me jewelry
Eve-ry gyal wan to have my baby
Beca me terrible good-lookin an me neva ugly
When me pickiny, me usee entertainer
Me usee chat lyric pon de corner
Beg likkle money from rich foreigna

Now me big bad, make a million dolla
Me hav one Toyota an one Maxima
One home New York, one home Jamaica
Champagne, Bubble Bath, Leather Sofa
With Gold Chain Pon Me Neck An Ring Pon Me
Finga!

Cease! Bally Shoe! Round of applause fe de people dem. I love you. Hug an kiss to each an every person. Me a de Madman! Always come 100 percent Gold Ring, Gold Chain, Gold Tooth. Bally Shoe! Hug an kiss! Love you!

DONA ANN McADAMS

KAZMIERCZACK

[Kazmierczack, handyman for this tenement building, comes to fix the stove in a tenant's apartment in the afternoon. He knocks on the door. No one answers. He sees a familiar face down the hall and waves.]

ANYA! YAKSHEMASH! Viglondash bardzo wadnye gishe. .....Dopshe, dopshe.

[She leaves. He tries the door again.]

Halo! Is Kazmierczack! .....Halo. Kazmierczack. .....Halo eh, you something broke? Something you break? Something you always never very good? Ah! Kazmierczack, Rama-me, coming you fix. Ah, I fix. Thank you.

[He enters the apartment.] What you break? Sink good, no good? Ah, good. I no fix. .....Ah? Cook? Never coming hahh? Only bad? Never this ahh? I look. [He goes to the stove.] Maybe you many cook. . . . Ah, is no good. I fix. . . . You many cook? .....Many cook you? .....You chodak cook? .....Chodak. .....Eh, chodak . . . dook dook dook. .....Ah, chicken. Never chicken cook? .....Ah. Is good. You bread cook? .....Bread? .....Ah, is good. America, bread, good. Never bad dollar money bread. . . . Ah, America—dollar, my Poland—zwodzhe. Dollar, zwodzhe is all mmm, eh. You wish pay money bread this one Key Food. You maybe, "Halo—can I please one bread?" This, "Thank you very Key Food bread you." My Poland you wish pay money bread, never good dollar. My Poland you wish pay money this automobile, good dollar, you wish pay money bread, bad dollar, is no good. . . . You look? [He motions to the steel putty in his hand.] After take ten, eleven minute put ahh, after make aghh! Is go aghh, metal, pa! Is good. .....You work? What you work? .....Teacher? Oh, I know teacher . . . this . . . small people. You teacher good money? .....Bad. My wife teacher, this small people. My Poland, teacher good money. America, teacher no money. Is no good. Never money teacher, all small people is go . . . ahhh! Is bad. .....You cat? .....Cat. Eh, cat . . . meow . . . Ah, cat. Kazmierczack never look you cat. Only look you cat . . . box. Cat go . . . ahhh. Ah. .....Two cat? Oh, bad. My wife . . . cat. One, small. Maybe, one week, after Kazmierczack finish this work, me go this home, for small ten eleven minute sleep me. This shoe go . . . ahh for . . . ah. Cat, one, small, my wife, coming this . . . ehha. Only maybe this one week, cat only always never smell very good. This one week, cat every . . . [Mimes throwing up.] Ahhhh. Only ahh. .....Ah, throw! Throw! This cat is throw, my shoe. After Kazmierczack finish this sleep. Me, go this . . . ah. Look shoe. "Ey, cat! Why you throw this my shoe?" Cat look me, "Ahh never this shoe throw nothing me you this." Is no good. .....Okay, I fix. Ah, maybe you stop fifteen sixteen minute for . . . hwooh. After come metal. Okay, I fix. You this bread cook, you this chodak cook—ah, chicken cook. Okay, thank you. Dozobachenia. [He exits.]

PAULA COURT

FLOE

[Floe, a cool sixteenish, sits with two friends and beats hip-hop into the wooden box to supply the music for his rhyme.]

IT'S THE MACK MOTHERFUCKIN', DADDY
Never catch me drivin' a caddy

I prefer like a 190E
Imported all the way from Germany

It's the *F* to the *L* to the *O* to the *E*
I tantalize to tickle your throat like Tetley tea

I terrorize, stuff tough trash talkers and bluff
tykes
Twist the wrist to grab the microphone and I
wear Nikes

Color green, style hi-top, to flex the hip-hop
Born to rip the shop and rock the spot like
nonstop, yo . . .

My rhymes are fat, fresh, dumb, dope, down,
and groovy
I'm terminatin' suckas like Schwarzenegger in
that movie

Sucker emcees I consume, my rhymes boom
I knew I was dope walkin' out my mother's womb

I'll kick you in the head with my Tims, so I could
squoosh ya
See ya on the street, punk, word up, I'll mush ya

I'm not a pusher, flowin' like a gusher
A fucked-up motherfucker and I live inside
Flatbush-uh

I'm makin' dynamite explode, I'm launchin'
rockets
I robbed George Jetson, stuck up Spacely Sprockets

My pockets stay fat, with pictures of the
presidents
I'm ricochet-bing-bing rockin' rhymes for all ya
residents

Of Brooklyn, Queens, Manhattan, and the Bronx
You paid your fifteen dollars, yo I coulda got y'all
comps

Every time I rhyme I leave mikes twisted and bent
Never been to Riker's Island, but I almost went

I'm out there murfin', not Papa Smurf and
Foamin' like a Nerf and yeah—I fucked your
girlfriend

I smoke suckas mad fast just like the crack
I drop more fuckin' bombs than Bush did on Iraq

I'm stacked and stacked, drink a forty of Similac
Never call me wack because yo, kid, I pack

A pistol, so it's no use holdin' your crystal
I'll shoot ya point-blank in the head, then fuck
your sister

I'll throw ya down and step on your head just like
a Ring Ding
Beat ya ass worse than they did in the Rodney
King thing

The rhymes I hit ya with, boy, they ain't no duds
The microphone's the trigger and boom, I'm
droppin' Scuds

Yeah, and ya don't stop, keep on till the break of
dawn and . . . [Freestyle]

[To his boys] Ah yeah, you like that, you like that. I fucked it up though. I made up the part about the Scuds yesterday. I was like tryin' to, you know, end on some boom shit but at the same time relate it to like current events. .....What? You can't have the sample after my verse, man. You already got it after his verse. .....'Cause, that shit is mad redundant. You don't know what the fuck you talkin' about.

.....A'ight fine, then have the sample after my verse, but then you can't have it after his. .....Oh my god, shut the fuck up. We ain't even make the demo yet. Wait till we drop the demo, get a record deal, then when you got cash in your pocket you'll shut the fuck up then. .....'Cause people are gonna listen to it and be like, "That shit is mad redundant." You *do* get money, 'cause you know you get a advance, right? Like I heard Wu-Tang Clan got like two hundred fifty thousand dollars *each* before the record even came out! Each yo, each, each! But watch, this be just the motherfucker to like, take that money and go buy like a five-hundred bag of Buddha and ten hookers and shit. .....'Cause you're stupid. Hey yo, I get that money, I'm goin' to college in two seconds, yup. 'Cause otherwise they just look at you like another dumb rapper and shit. You got a degree in your pocket, niggas give you respect. For real, I'm gonna roll up like Harvard or Yale or some shit. Yo, there's mad honeys at them schools too yo. .....Nah, bee, you don't need SATs to get into that shit. .....Nah yo. I roll up in Harvard, a hundred thousand dollars in my pocket, they be like, "A'ight, you in, you in." Trust me. They be like, "Oh hello, welcome" and shit.

.....What? You don't know what the fuck you're talkin' about. You can't even rhyme for shit anyway. Aha! .....My mother can't rhyme? Yo, your mother's so stupid, she climbed up a tree 'cause she tryin' to be branch manager. .....Yo, your mother's so dumb, she got stabbed in a shootout. .....Hah? .....Oh, why you wanna go there, man? .....I'm sayin', you dis my moms all you want, but you don't talk about my girl, that's different. .....I know she ain't my girl no more, that's not the point though. .....Yo, we broke up, you don't even know the whole story. .....Nah, I'm sayin', she wanna go roll with some other kid 'cause he got money in his pocket. That's a'ight though. 'Cause wait till we get this record deal and I got money in my pocket, you know she gonna be callin' me up like, ring ring, "Hi, I'm sorry." I'll be like, "Word?" Click. .....Nah, actually I can't say that. 'Cause she ain't really the type to do that shit. See, that's why I can't dis her even though we broke up. I mean out of all the girls I been with, I be like, "See ya!" But it's like that's the first girl that like, I don't know. I think honestly I could say like . . . I don't know . . . some shit.

.....Nah! I'm serious! It's like, even just being with her, we don't even have to be doing nothing, we just be sitting there. Plus she be schooling me, 'cause you know she's in college, right? She's gonna be a sophomore at Hunter next semester. .....Black and Puerto Rican studies. So I'm sayin', it's like we just be chilling or whatever. And all of the sudden she'll drop the bomb of knowledge on me. Like check this out, there was this whole civilization, livin' on the islands in the Caribbean, mad hundred thousand years before the Europeans came over and fucked that whole shit up. They was called Tainos.

They had a whole civilization, architecture, medicine, culture .....Tainos. .....You ain't never heard of no fuckin' Tainos. This nigga ain't never heard of Fritos talkin' 'bout you heard of that shit. I'm sayin' though, shit was just different with her. .....That too though. It's like, even when I was fuckin' her. Ah, see I can't even say that 'cause it wasn't like fuckin'. It was like we was making love or some shit. .....Shut up. Stop laughing. Your mother's so fat she jumped in the air and got stuck, shut the fuck up. .....Nah, shut the fuck up, stop laughing though. I'm saying, I'm gonna tell you this 'cause it still be buggin' me out to this day. This happened like once, right? .....I'm not saying I fucked her once, but listen. You know when you be gettin' busy, and like you get all into the moment and shit? Like you get all hot and sweaty and you get into the smells, like you be smelling her neck and shit. You know, you be like, "Ah, lemme smell your neck"? So, I'm saying like one time, we was all in it. And I had closed my eyes and this shit had come over me like I can't even explain it. Like in here, and I had like almost started like, cryin' and shit. I mean I'm not saying I was crying. I'm saying like, a'ight. The only thing I could compare it to is, remember last summer we went to Action Park? .....Nah, a'ight, bad example, bad example.

I'm sayin', you ever been on a airplane? .....So you know you be on a airplane and you hit turbulence and the plane drops? And your stomach goes like this, but the rest of your body goes like this? . . . It's like you're separating and you feel like . . . I'm saying, so they got that water slide at Action Park, and when you go down the slide you be like . . . wahh. I'm not sayin' down there, I'm saying like in here. .....Never mind, man. .....Nah, forget it, shut up, you're stupid. Watch in like five years, she'll be some college professor, and we'll be on tour at her school. And we'll run into each other and be like, ching! . . . Nah yo, let me shut up, man. I be sounding all sentimental like Sally Jeffrey Rafael and shit. Yo, kick your verse, man, kick your verse! Ya big, can't rhyme for your life. .....What? Yo, your mother got no arms on *Wheel of Fortune,* talkin' 'bout—"Big Money! Big Money!" [Floe pounds the box to his homeboy's imaginary verse.]

DONA ANN McADAMS

BILL

[A straight-outta-Jersey pseudo-yuppie with a Jeep runs up to his friend's apartment with him for a would-be two minutes. Bill talks while his friend struggles with the many locks on the door.]

.....ALL RIGHT, BUT JUST FOR TWO minutes because my Jeep is double-parked downstairs and I don't want to get tickets. Can I tell you what your problem is? And this is your problem because I know because I'm very good at telling things about people. You, you don't pay attention to things that are going on around you. It's like you're in this shell. You're like this turtle, you know, crawling along the grass in your shell and bombs are dropping like five centimeters away from you. And you, you're in la-la land. You're like, la-la. Can I give you an example? Let me give you a perfect example. Did you watch Ted Koppel last week? .....Okay, well, if you would've watched, you would've known that there's little nine-year-olds running around the street with guns, selling crack to babies for sex. .....You think I'm exaggerating? If you would've watched, you would've known. You also would've known, get this: There's some guy, he killed all these hookers, right? You know, prostitutes? Killed them. But this is the thing, there are all these people and they're in this rage that he shouldn't have killed them. Lemme tell you something, if he didn't kill them they would've wound up spreading AIDS to half the people in this country. .....Because this is a very serious issue of our time and it affects us all indirectly.

.....Okay, I'll give you a perfect example. Let's say, some guy he makes a mistake. Not me, but some guy. He goes and uses a prostitute, right? She gives him AIDS, 'cause she's got AIDS, she gives it to him, he goes home to his wife, he gives it to her, she has no idea. Are you following the progression of the story? Then they get a divorce, because of course they're gonna get a divorce because why is the guy with the . . . Anyway, she's out there, you know, on the single scene, whatever you wanna call it. I'm thirty-five years old, I'm a single man. I meet her, she gives me AIDS, I'm dead. You're asking how it affects me? .....Use a condom? I'm thirty-five years old, I think I'm a little old to use a condom, anyway you're missing the whole point of the story. Listen, I thought we're coming up here for two minutes so you could shave, this is turning into a whole ordeal here with getting into your apartment. What's with the five locks on your door, what are we in Harlem? Heh . . . It's a joke, you got five locks on your door, you know, Harlem, it's all these people up there? .....All right, so it's not funny, so now you're a Black Panther all of the sudden? Jesus, it's a joke. Mr. Medeco here. You make me very uncomfortable sometimes.

[Bill enters apartment.] Oh, this is nice. .....I said this is nice, your place. How much do you pay for this? .....Not bad. Who's the guy that owns the building? The same guy that owns the building on the corner? What's his name? .....Mohammed? Is he Moroccan? .....But is he Moroccan? .....Yeah, but is he Moroccan though? .....No, I bet he's Moroccan. Because all the Moroccans, they bought up all the real estate, from the Jews. .....No, yes, trust me. They did a whole in-depth report on *MacNeil-Lehrer,* I saw the whole thing. You didn't know the Jews are going poor? Not just that they had to sell . . . Trust me—my friend who's Jewish, he wanted to get for his daughter—what do you call it when they get their own . . . her own phone line—he couldn't get it for her, that's all I'm saying. Anyway that's not the point of the story. The point of the story is that all the Moroccans bought up all the real estate, and all the Baskin-Robbins. And I don't know this just because I watch TV and I'm socially aware, paying attention unlike you—you're in la-la land—but I know this from empirical observation. I was in a Baskin-Robbins last month and I'm standing there paying for the cone, and I ask the guy his name. You know I'm always taking advantage of these little small-talk opportunities, you get to know people really well. So the guy says Mohammed. .....The guy's Moroccan, so he's Moroccan, Libyan, Hindu, Iraqi. They're all connected. They're all in the same little boat there.

Let me ask you something, do you watch Dan Rather? From now on, you have to watch Dan Rather just for educational purposes. Because on Dan Rather, you get the whole complete story. Let me explain something to you. They got this whole Shiite cult, the Buddhists, right? And the thing is they name them all Mohammed so they can't tell the difference between each other. It's like brainwashing. They're brainwashing them into thinking that they're all this one common organism floating around the earth, and they're gonna take over other organisms, and the other ones are innocent law-abiding countries, like ours. I mean they didn't say that exactly on Dan Rather, but you could figure it all out. The Shiites are sort of like the Moonies, it's all interwoven. Anyway that's not the point, the point is just be careful there's not a bomb in your building. You think these guys got real estate on their minds? I'm thinking not. . . . Where'd you get this, Ikea? .....This table thing here, I thought it was Ikea. Heh.

Listen, hurry up, because if I got tickets on my Jeep you're paying for them. Hey, you know I'm thirty-five, right? Yeah, I turned thirty-five last week. .....Thank you, thank you. Anyway, you know I'm old enough to be president, right? You know what I'd do if I was president? You know, to solve all the problems, hatred, racism, killing, stuff? Now keep in mind I'm not prejudice or anything. I'd teach everybody how to speak English. Because that's the problem. I mean, if you don't speak English, how are we supposed to communicate for, you know, peace? Let me give you a perfect example. The other day I finish work, I'm hungry, I feel like having Chinese food. So I go to the Chinese take-out in my neighborhood, I order what I always order—four fried chicken wings, it comes with a small roast pork fried rice. So this day, me, I'm feeling hungrier than normal, so I order a large roast pork fried rice instead of a small, you know? I'll pay for it. So I say to the guy, "Can I have a large instead of a small?" So the guy goes yeah, like he understands what I'm saying. Mistake Number One, the guy doesn't know what the hell I'm saying. You wanna hear Mistake Number Two? Me, I'm looking out the window making sure my Jeep isn't getting ripped off by, you know, crackhead murderers in the street. Meanwhile, I should be watching, who knows what the hell they're putting in my food? Poison, whatever. .....You don't know what they put in, they have their little jars of stuff next to the woks. So that's not even the thing. This is the thing. The guy goes to put it in the bag with the duck sauce and everything. Get this, he puts it in the bag behind the counter. So you can't really see what he's putting in the bag, it could be a bomb. .....You're laughing? You're very unaware.

Can I just tell you, *20/20* did a whole four-part series on bombings, and Barbara was explaining that these bombs went off and nobody would have ever guessed that there was a bomb. .....Then why do they put it in the bag behind the counter then? They got a whole top of the counter, the top of the counter's clean. Everything is behind the counter, behind the counter. .....They're very sneaky. So the moral of the story is, I take the bag, I drive all the way home, four blocks. Meanwhile, I could blow up on the way home. I sit down, I take off my shoes, I turn on the TV. I wanna relax, you know. I worked hard all day, I don't know about *these* people. I open the bag, they gave me a small— .....A small roast pork fried rice . . . are you listening to the story? All right. So me, I'm angry. I'm flustered. I'm looking into the bag and it's like looking into this tunnel of frustration and anger. So I put it back in the bag, I drive all the way back, four blocks, so now it's eight blocks I've driven for this thing already.

I walk in to the guy, see now the guy's not there anymore. Now it's his sister, or his mother, or his wife, his aunt . . . they're all in the family there. .....Because I know, because I know. So I say to her, "Look, I ordered a large, you gave me a small." So she says, "What?" Already we're having miscommunication. So I tell her, "I. Want. A. Large." She says, "Two-fifty." I say, "No, no, hello, before, earlier . . ." I'm trying to think of all the possible adjectives, I'm like a thesaurus. You know— "Prior to the time when I'm standing before you here now, I already—*then*—ordered a large. You made a mistake." You know, I mean I'm a man, I'm thirty-five years old, I'm not a kid. I want service, you know? So she's going, "Dut dut dut dut dut dut dut dut dut." Like I'm supposed to understand what she's saying? She's supposed to understand *me,* thank you! So then she turns to her brother or her husband or her uncle— .....Because just trust me, they are, I know the people in my neighborhood. And she's saying something to him very fast. So I'm trying to listen to what she's saying, she's telling him to blow me up for all I know. So then, 'cause I'm listening, 'cause I'm a listener, I hear her say this thing and I recorded it in my brain and I want to do it for you so shut off the water. She says, "Something something," and then she says, "beaow." What does that mean? That's not a normal sound. .....Because I went to college, I have a master's degree in business, thank you, I think I know a little something about languages if you give me the benefit of the doubt.

Look, the point of the story is this, these people have got to go through some sort of assimilation program before they come to this country so they can, a) learn how to speak English, and b) learn how to function like normal human beings, like us. .....Because how are you gonna run a business and not speak English? Look at the guy who owns the 7-Elevens, he's from India, he learned how to speak it. Look at the American Indians, they learned to speak it when they came over here. But see these people, they come from out of nowhere, and in twenty-four hours they get a license to open a restaurant. That's like giving a woman a license . . . to fix trucks. I mean not that I'm saying women can't fix trucks, it's just . . . I don't really know what I'm saying actually. The bottom line is this, if you took all these people, from the cleaning people, the nannies, and the maintenance people, the housekeepers, and the kitchens, the guys that work at the place where I get my Jeep washed. If you took all of them and you sent them back to all of their little terrorist countries, we wouldn't have all this suffering here and just, things wouldn't be as hard.

.....Trust me, I'll get somebody to wash it, there'll be somebody. Oh, you have a cat. I didn't see before. It must have just come out from wherever it was. That's funny how all of the sudden they just decide to run out of nowhere. You don't seem like the cat type. You know it's my favorite animal? Is it a Persian? .....I bet its name is Mohammed. Hi, kitty cat. Hiya, ya big cutie. Ooh too too. What are you looking at? What are you doing? Where are you going? Ooh too too. Moo moo mama. Come here, cutie. I'm gonna get you. I'm gonna get you. [He picks up the cat.] . . . Oh, I got you. Oh. I. Got. You. Oh, you're so heavy, you little small kitty cat. Let's go look in the mirror. Oh, look in that mirror. Look. In. That. Mirror. Who's that guy behind you? "I don't know. Some guy." Gimme that paw. Gimme that paw. Lemme see that paw. How you doing? "I'm okay." Hah. Oh ribbit ribbit. Moo. Gobble gobble. Meow . . . [He abruptly drops the cat.] Look at all this shit I got all over me now. Listen, I'm going downstairs. I got a hundred and fifty tickets on my Jeep already, or they towed it. .....Trust me, they're giving out tickets. I just read they hired all these *whatever* meter maids, all they do is hand out tickets all day. .....Because I read it. What do you think, they write it for nothing? These guys they got this whole thing connected to those hate groups that were on *60 Minutes*. What they do these guys, they see my Jeep, they see the Jersey plate, automatically they assume that I'm white. I mean I am, but that's not the point. The point is that they think that Jersey's all white people. Let me tell you, it's not. You come to my neighborhood, I gotta get five locks on my door. Listen, I'll see ya downstairs. [Bill exits.]

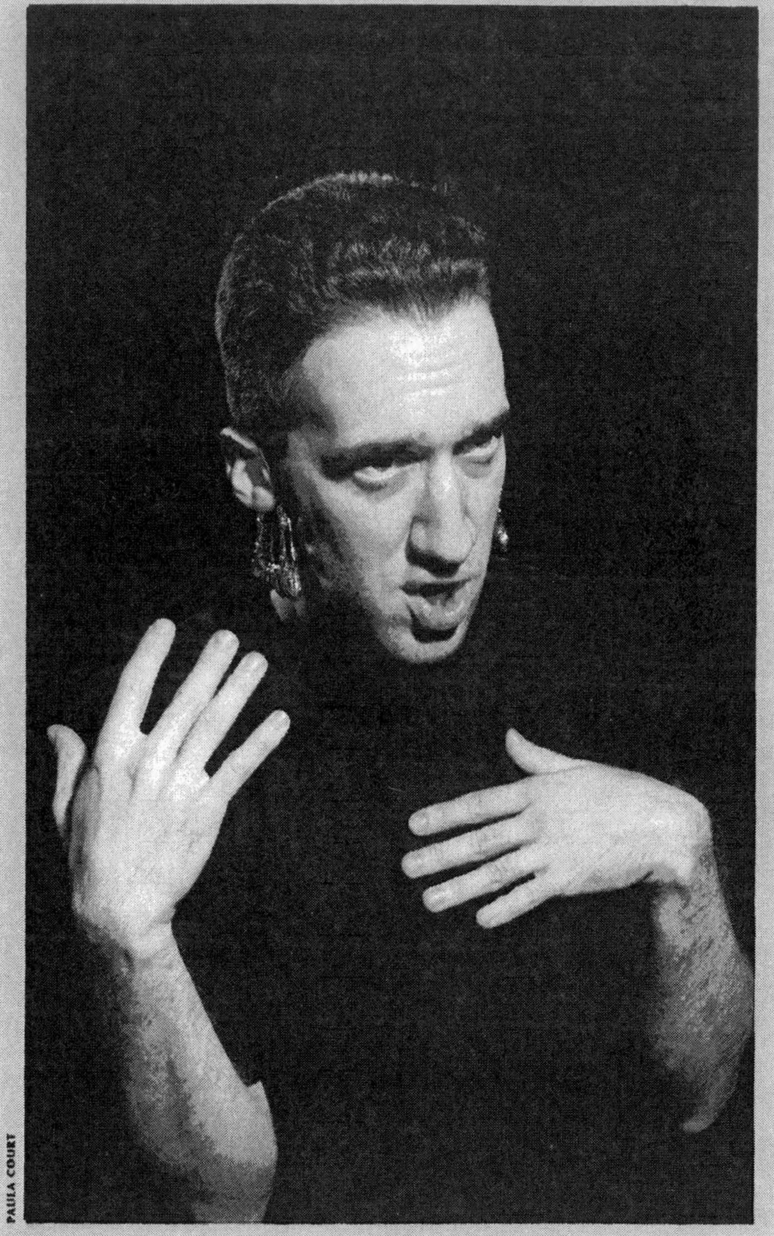

PAULA COURT

BLANCA

[Blanca, a young twenty-something office worker, stops by her friend's house to borrow shoes.]

LISTEN, LISETTE, LEMME BORROW your shoes? The short black ones. .....No, because Manny gets off Foot Locker in twenty minutes and I have to take the bus. .....But I can't be looking ugly in the bus. .....So find them! Don't stress me more, all right? My life is already stressed enough, can I tell you? The other day, right? I was at Manny's house, and we was fooling around, and like you know how guys be getting all shy like when they wanna say something really important but they don't say it? Or like they say it, but like their voices be getting all low so you can't hear what they saying? So he was doing that, right, and like I don't be playing that. I was like, "Hello-excuse-me-I-can't-hear-you-what-you-saying," right?

So I figure he's doing that because he wants to ask me to marry him 'cause already we been together one year nine months seventeen days and he ain't asked me nothing. So I look, and he got this thing behind his back, and I figure it's a Hallmark card or something saying like, "Hello Blanca how you doing I love you will you marry me?" Instead, he got a condom, right? .....Right? So I was like, "Excuse me, who's that for?" He was like, "That's for us." I was like, "Excuse me, I do not think that's for us." But he goes, "No, we have to use it," because he said that he had seen some thing in like Channel 13 or something, like some thing. He goes, "No, you have to be careful, you don't know what's out there." I was like, "Excuse me, I know what's out there, I'm talking about what's in here," right? I was like, "You ain't sticking no fucking rubber shit up inside me I don't know who touched it. You might as well put a rubber glove and do some Spic and Span in that shit, 'cause I ain't having that." .....No, 'cause one year nine months seventeen days we been together, now he comes to me with it? *Now* he thinks I'm dirty? I ain't fucking dirty.

And he thinks like I don't know nothing. Like he thought that I thought that you could get it from mosquitoes. Plus it ain't like I just met him. I know his whole family, his parents, his sisters. They're nice people. If I would have got something, I would have got it one year nine months seventeen days ago, right? .....No, we talked about it, but you think we used it? . . . We started fooling around, I was like, "You seen *this* in Channel 13?" He was like, "No." I was like, "Mmm-hmm."

.....Not those, the black ones you wore last Friday! The short ones with the bows on it. I'm telling you though, Manny be driving me crazy sometimes for the dumb reasons. Like, you know Manny's father's Puerto Rican and his mother's Spanish. So he's Puerto Rican, right? And he's dark and his last name is Sorullo. So when people ask him, he always says Sorulo. 'Cause he says he wants to work in business in Wall Street, and that nobody wants to hire a Sorullo. So I be telling him, "Manny, that's your last name, you can't do that." And he be getting angry at me like, "That's my last name, that's how it's pronounced!" And like, "You got it easier than me, Blanca, 'cause you're lighter than me, 'cause you're a woman." And I'm like, "Excuse me, I'm Puerto Rican too," right? So it was the Puerto Rican Day Parade, and I had gotten us these T-shirts with the Puerto Rican flag in the front, and in the back there's a little coquí and it says "Boricua and Proud." So you would think that he would be like, "Oh, thank you, Blanca, that's so sweet, I love you," right? Instead he starts screaming, "I'm not wearing this shit! I can't believe you got me this! It's ugly!" I was like, "Excuse me, it's not ugly." So he puts on a Ralph Lauren shirt. I was like, "Manny, you think somebody's hiring you for Wall Street at the Puerto Rican Day Parade?" So he goes to me, "Look, Blanca, I might be Puerto Rican, but I don't have to walk around looking like one." . . . I was like, "Excuse me. You think that people think that you Swedish? You Puerto Rican." I couldn't believe it. It's like, he wants to wear a condom, but not a T-shirt.

.....Not those ugly heels, the short ones with the bows. .....So find them, don't stress me more! It's like I be nice to people and they be having temper tantrums. You're like Lemington. You know my roommate Lemington, right? .....I know, his name is Lemington, that's weird, right? So you know he's gay, right? And you know if you see Lemington, you be like, "Oh my god this guy is gay." But if you see his boyfriend, you be like, "Oh my god this guy is not gay." 'Cause he's like six foot and all muscular. Like when I first had seen him I was like, "Mmm." Like that, right? But he's gay. And they're not only gay, they're black and gay. Can you believe that? I couldn't believe that. .....No, 'cause they don't look like those guys from *In Living Color.* At all. But you know I don't care 'cause I'm very liberal. But I think that his boyfriend be beating him 'cause one day Lemington had a cut right here, and I seen those signs in the subway that like if you're gay and your lover beats you call that number. ......Right . . . whatever.

So we be getting along, except this one morning I'm getting ready to go to work. It's like seven-thirty in the morning and I'm sitting there eating breakfast, I look up and he's wearing my skirt. So I was like, "Lemington, what you doing with my skirt?" He was like, "That's your skirt?" I was like, "Yes, that's my skirt, Lemington, where you got it?" He goes, "In the closet." I was like, "Well that would happen to be my closet, which would happen to be in my room, so that would happen to be—ding!—my skirt," right? I was like, "Lemington, you can't be wearing my skirt." So he starts crying, right? And he's like, "Fine, I won't wear it!" And I can't have him crying in my house at seven-thirty in the morning 'cause then the neighbors be thinking like *I'm* beating him or something, right? So we had gotten over it, right? Except that he be leaving me these pamphlets all over the house. Like in the dishes he puts them, in the freezer. So, should I go to get a ice cube, I'll read a pamphlet. Meanwhile I got frozen pamphlets in the freezer. It's this one pamphlet, it's called "Getting to Know Your Body." It's these drawings of these women, looking at themselves, in you know, there, with instructions. Excuse me, but I don't need to be looking there. For what? It's money in there? Plus, what if somebody comes over and they go to get a ice cube, they'll be thinking that I'm looking in there with instructions like, what's this? He thinks that I'm like one of these women that doesn't know nothing about her body and goes and does whatever. [She puts on some lipstick.]

But he's sweet though, he got me this cute shirt with all these pictures of famous womens on it. Clara Barton, Nefertiti, Mother Teresa is on the shirt. And he gives it to me and he goes to me, "Rejoice in your womanhood, Blanca, be good to yourself 'cause you're a warrior." I was like, this is some black gay thing or something? He called me a warrior. I picture myself like running through the jungle with a machine gun like, "Look out, it's Blanca coming!"

But the thing is, now he got this little dog, right? And a) he don't be feeding it, so the dog be eating my curtains, now I don't have no curtains people could just be looking at me naked through the window. And b) he don't walk it. So the dog be shitting all in my house. And let me tell you, I don't know what the dog be shitting because it got nothing to eat but curtains. It's like little curtain shits is in the floor. The other day I'm getting ready to go to work and I get out the shower in my towel, I step in this little macadamia nut shit. So he goes, "Wipe it." So I wipe it, I took a Bounty but I don't have time to go back in the shower and scrubbing shit out my foot twenty-four hours. So I go to work. People at work are like, "Ooh you smell like shit." And when I explain to them that, "Excuse me, I do not smell like shit naturally, but I happened to *step* in shit," they're like, "Oh, you stepped in shit? You must be stupid then." And I'll tell you right now, I can't have people calling me stupid, 'cause I ain't stupid.

.....No, I wanna kick him out, but then he'll think it's 'cause he's gay. I mean it's not that he's gay that his dog shits in the floor, it's that he's irresponsible. Things are so complicated. Plus I think he got AIDS too, 'cause he's all skinny. .....Yeah, Manny's skinny too, but Manny's just skinny. Lemington's gay and skinny, all right? . . . But them people be getting that shit anyway, right? .....They do though, right? .....Right. You got them? Finally, gimme. I hope they fit. I'm telling you, you know what is it? [Blanca puts on the shoes and checks herself in the mirror.] I think my life is stressed because I have to learn to be nice to myself. 'Cause if you think about it, nobody's being nice to me. You included. But listen, I have to go because you making me late. And these shoes are too tight but I'm wearing them. And let me tell you something. If Manny comes to me with that whole condom thing again, I'm gonna tell him like this, "You think I'm dirty? Who do you think I am? Do you even know who *you* are?"

PAULA COURT

AL CAPÓN

[Al Capón is a fast-paced disc jockey and radio personality. He is the Latin American/ Spanish-speaking counterpart of Caribbean Tiger. The stage is dimly lit and he races from time and weather to live advertisements with quick merengue interludes.]

ANDANDO! HOLY MOLY Guacamole mis amigos. Tenemos las doce y treinta minutos y estámos con el super éxito de Toño Rosario! Wow! Yo soy Adalberto Capón, mejor conocido a ustedes, Al Capón. Aquí estoy en tu SuperPoderosa FM 99. Holy Moly Guacamole, la temperatura afuera está de veinticinco grados entonces, cuídanse mucho que no cojan gripe porque hay muchas mongas afuera que coger! Okay okay okay Cambio! [Music]

Este Sábado el 2000 Club presenta directamente de Santo Domingo la capital del merengue, Jossie Esteban y La Patrulla 15. Las mujeres entran gratis! Gratis! Gratis! Antes de las once. Otra vez, Jossie Esteban y La Patrulla 15 Este Sábado en el 2000 Club en la calle 177 y Broadway en el alto Manhattan! El 2000 Club!

Okay okay okay. Este segmento de música de quince minutos está presentado por Kool-Aid. Kool-Aid Kool-Aid Kool-Aid. Disponible en todos los sabores que te encantarán. Como SuperCherry, SuperGrape, SuperStrawberry y FunkyFruit! Okay okay okay. Kool-Aid Kool-Aid Kool-Aid. Andando! [Music]

Este fin de semana en el Gigantic Tomato Supermarket en Brentwood, Long Island! La SuperVenta del Siglo—Holy Moly! Muslos de pollo Shady Brook Farms—noventa y nueve centavos por libra! Plátanos SuperVerdes—nueve por un dólar! Sweetpotato sweetpotato marca Gran Batata—setenta y nueve centavos por libra! Holy Moly I can't believe it! Este fin de semana en el Gigantic Tomato Supermarket en Brentwood, Long Island!

Okay okay okay mis amigos aquí estamos en la capital del mundo, Nueva York. Y estamos con, "Happy birthday to you, happy birthday to you, happy birthday dear . . . Isabel Santiago del Bronx, happy birthday to you." Okay okay okay. Muchas felicidades a usted Isabel Santiago del Bronx de su esposo Manny Santiago, allá en el Bronx también por supuesto.

Okay okay okay. Si tú eres good-looking, o si tú eres looking good, call me baby. Porque yo no soy alcapurria, yo soy Al Capón, aquí en tu SuperPoderosa Hot FM 99. Holy Moly Guacamole mis amigos! Andando! [Music]

PAULA COURT

DORIS

[Doris, a mother of one in her fifties, is in her kitchen, using her power tool, the phone, to communicate with some people, while her husband fixes something in another room.]

.....WILL YOU SHUSH?! .....SO SHAH! Martin, the guy is coming in five minutes. So leave the thing alone! In five minutes he'll be here and he'll fix the whole thing. .....I know the phone is ringing, I'm letting it ring. .....So let me let it ring!

Hello? Who is this? .....Who? .....Oh, hi! How are you? .....No, what are you interrupting? You're interrupting nothing. .....Uy, no, no. I'm sitting here, I'm— .....What wire, Martin? What wire? I'm supposed to know what wire you're talking about? Oh, that wire, sure. Keep futzing with the wire and blow yourself up. You're not blowing me up!

.....No, I'm fine. Martin's fine. David's fine. Yeah, in fact, I'm supposed to call my sonny boy in five minutes, so I'll talk quick. .....No, no he's fine. How's your daughter? .....Gonna marry to who? Not the same Nigerian guy? .....Does she love him? .....So, she loves him and she'll be happy and they'll be happy. Listen, did she make sure he's all tested with all whatever he needs with shots and everything? .....No, I'm just saying, because especially with he's from Africa, she should make sure, 'cause I saw in the *Times*. .....How terrible. Isn't it?

.....He's a doctor, the guy? And he's from Nigeria? .....Eh, well still. .....No, he doesn't see her anymore. Eh, Roz, to tell you the truth, I had a bad feeling about her when I first met her. She's a sweet girl, and she's attractive, but there was something creepy about her. She had a creepy aura. Anyway. Did I tell you what he's doing now, my son? .....Oh Roz, he goes with this group of people and they go into all the bad neighborhoods, and I gotta tell ya, I am so— .....Yeah, I think it's like the Peace Corps, but in New York. .....Who? David? Hold on, let me ask . . .

Martin! Does David get insurance with the job? .....David your son. Does he get insurance with the job, the thing with the— .....Never mind, you're not understanding me. .....You're not understanding me, never mind! [To Roz] Listen, I'll ask him when I'll call him. Listen, mameleh, I gotta go, darling, okay? I'll call you back after. Okay, bye.

[She clicks the phone only to make another call.] Martin! How do I do the memory with the phone, I forgot? .....The memory, for David, I know I put for number one, but after I do the star button or before? .....The pound button? There's no pound button, Martin. .....There's no pound button, I'm looking at the phone! Uch, I'm doing the star! .....All right, shush, it's ringing! It's ringing and I can't hear! Will you keep with the wires, keep breaking the thing more, more break it!

.....Hello, David, sweetheart, it's your mommyface, listen—Hello? Hi, you're there? .....So what are you screening your phone calls, someone's after you? .....So pick up the phone, it's your mother calling, it's a secret that you're there? .....Uch, you make me nervous with this machine, one day I'll call it'll say, "Hi, this is David, I'm not here from they killed me on the train" or wherever. .....All right, I'm relaxed, I just worry with you in all these . . . uch. .....Yes, David, but not everyone takes the trains by theirself to the South Bronx or wherever. Sure the people that live there, but they're different . . . I mean not that they're different, they're the same as us, everyone is the same, but, all right, never mind, it's just different, you don't get it, forget it. You can't take a cab sometimes? .....So let everybody else take the train, you're not them, you have to do what they do? All right, I'm relaxed.

Anyway, bubbeleh, what I wanna ask ya . . . Does your job, do they give you health insurance? .....So you'll pay the ten dollars and you'll have it. How much more? .....That's ridiculous, are you sure? .....All right, so I'll pay it. David, I'm not an extravagant person that I'm saving for a yacht, I'll be happy to pay for it. Or if you want you could go on the plan your father and I have, hold on . . .

Martin! What's the deductible on the insurance? What's that noise? Now you're drilling? What are you drilling? The guy is coming, Martin! .....The deductible! On the Blue Cross, the Blue Cross! .....That's what I'm asking you, how much?! .....Uh, forget it. Forget! It! . . . Listen, David honey, we'll call the 1-800— .....Wait, I'm on the phone with David! [To David] Hello? [To Martin] *"Which David?!"* [To David] Uch, wait one second.

Martin! When the guy comes for the thing, you're staying with him, right? .....What do you mean you're going for a walk? Martin, I'm not letting these people into my house I don't know who they are, the minorities or whoever. . . . [To David] Uy, you hear this from your father? Where is he walking? In front of a truck he'll walk. .....You're right, David, they could be anybody. They could be Jewish, whoever, I'm just saying I'm not staying here alone. While he'll be going for a walk they'll be drilling me in the head for the television. .....All right. David. I said they didn't have to be minorities. Uy, you're such a mensch, you're a sweetheart, you're very caring, I'm very proud of you, mmwa! So listen, tateleh, do you wanna do with the Blue Cross? .....What no? Everyone has to have health insurance, David. .....So fine, thirty-six percent of the country doesn't have it, you're not thirty-six percent, you're my son. .....So David, let the thirty-six percent sit for ten hours waiting in some dirty emergency room somewhere bleeding to death with flies and urine and five hundred sick people with tuberculosis.

.....My son . . . my son is not gonna sit waiting in some clinic full of people's phlegm all over the floor and everyone's coughing with no air. .....No, David. God forbid. . . . David, God forbid I should be concerned already enough that my son doesn't get shot by some black kid, *or white kid,* in one of these places, but that he should go to a professional Jewish hospital?. .....I know white people shoot people with guns, David, but . . . in other countries. .....David look, I know I raised you to believe that everyone's equal, and not to be into materials, and to accept people no matter who they are, but David, I am your mother and I know you're an adult, but there are some things about reality that you're not understanding. .....I can't be concerned about my son? .....I'm not the one yelling, you're yelling! I just want you to be happy and not dead.

David, don't hang up, I want to talk to you. I am proud of you. I brag to all my friends and they all can't believe it. They all say, "I can't believe it." Is it too much to ask for you to have health insurance? .....How do you know nothing'll happen? You have a crystal ball? .....David, they'll have one of their riots these people and you'll be the first one they'll shoot. .....They shoot people, David, I read *The New York Times.* Not the *Post,* the *Times,* and I see them. They shoot each other. And let me tell you something, David, I feel very bad. I wish these kids didn't have to grow up with all violence and uch, a mess, and my heart goes out to them, it does, but let them shoot each other and not you, that's the way I feel.

.....I am not racist, David! Don't you dare call me racist! Because if you remember, I let you have all your black and Puerto Rican and Iranian friends at your bar mitzvah, and I treated them just like I treated your Jewish friends. You wanna see racist? Go read with this guy in the paper, "Bloodsuckers," he said. .....I am not a "Scared-Liberal-Complaining-Reactionary." What does that mean? When they'll wanna stick you in an oven, you'll still defend this guy? You wanna be another martyr, David? You wanna be one of the Jewish kids in Mississippi with the voter registration and they killed them, them and some black guy? .....How is it possible for Jews to be prejudice when everyone is prejudice all the time against the Jews? David, we had lots of black neighbors before we moved, and we got along fine. My friend Roz's daughter Cynthia is marrying a Nigerian guy and he's a doctor! .....No, David, the difference is, did I call them bloodsuckers? I said they shoot people, I didn't call names.

.....How am I guilty? I'm guilty of reading *The New York Times*? David, how come you'll never defend the Jews? You're Jewish but you'll never empathize with your own people. ....."What is there to empathize?" David, six million—did you see *Schindler's List*? The Jews are still victims. .....How am I a victim in the suburbs in 1994? .....Not because I have a juicer and an espresso machine makes me a vict— Black people have juicers and espresso makers too! What are you screaming? What bad thing did I do? I did something bad to them? David, I'm not crazy. You ask people if they'll be in these neighborhoods on the train. .....Whatever people. You ask them if they'll defend this guy. .....The black kid who's in jail for murder I should defend? For what? Where do you get this from? Why are you so angry? You're not even black! Why are you angry at your own people? Why are you so angry at me? I'm your mother!

Uy, all right, calm down. Stop yelling! Listen to me. Are you still coming to the seder on Thursday? Your Aunt Barbara's coming and so is your cousin Mark. Mark, the high school principal, gay Mark. And I promise I won't start an argument with you, or Mark. .....Okay, stop yelling. Are you coming? .....Well if you don't I'll be very upset. Fine, listen, I'm not angry at you. Are you angry at me? All right, well, it's all right, I'm your mother. Okay, I love you. Bye. .....Okay, stop screaming. .....Okay, bye, mmwa! [Doris hangs up the phone.] Martin . . . I'm going for a walk.

PAULA COURT

FLEX

[Flex, nineteen, pants sagging, Timbos dragging, five beepers and a chewstick. He approaches a Chinese take-out restaurant rapping to a song on his Walkman. He enters and stands next to another customer.]

HEY YO, YOU ON LINE? A'ight then. [Flex looks up at the picture menus on the wall above his head. To the restaurant guy] Hey yo, I'm still lookin', man. Damn, man, niggas try to rush me, man. [He takes a moment to ponder his order.] . . . Hey yo, Chinaman! Chinaman! Yo Chinese yo! Lemme get Number Seven yo. .....Number Seven! Hey yo, I ain't look on there yo, I'm lookin' right there! Niggas got signs up, don't know what the fuck they got up. .....Hah? Oh, vegetable lo mein? Oh, I ain't see that right there, goodlookin'. Yo, vegetable lo mein, son, small. Small, you know what I'm sayin' small? Small! .....Hey yo my man, no mushrooms, no onions in that yo. .....Mushrooms, you know mushrooms? No mushrooms. And no onion. .....Onions! You know what a onion is? I don't eat that shit. I'ma tell you what, I find mushrooms and onions in that shit, you could take that shit back, word up. Hey yo son, how long yo? How long? How long? .....Right, I'ma be back then.

[Flex exits to street and sees an old friend.] Oh shit! Wasup, kid? Oh my god! It's the god! It's the god right now. It's that nigga Al! Oh snap. Wasup with you, man? Goddamn. I ain't seen you in the longest time. What you been up to? .....Word? I hear dat, I hear dat. .....Nuttin' man, I'm about to get some food in here right quick, go pick up my little brother from school. Hey yo, it's good to see you, man. Hey yo, check this, I got five beepers, kid, you think I'm lyin'? Check them shits, boy. One, two, three, four, boom! What you wanna do 'bout that? These four are like regular, they go like, beep, beep. But this joint right here, this shit go like this, ooh-ooh! Shit's all disco-style. You should hang out with me for a while and you could hear that shit go off. Hey yo, so what you up to lately, kid? What you gonna do next year though? .....Get the fuck outta here! Scholarship? See that's 'cause you all on that brainiac tip.

You thought I forgot. I don't forget shit, boy. Remember we used to be in school, and we used to be in the library throwin' shit and the teacher used to come by and we'd be like . . . But you was really readin' that shit though, right? So what you gonna study? You gonna study business, right? My man gonna make mad loot in this piece! .....Black history? My man said black history yo. Tah-ha. This nigga buggin' yo! Oh shit— [He mimes staring at a book.] "Harriet Tubman, Freedom Fighter." Your ass gonna be broke as hell beggin' in the street and whatnot. .....Nah, I don't mean to break, man, you get mad props for that shit, you get respect. Somebody gotta do that shit, right? I'm sayin' though, I gotta get that loot, son, word is bond. I'm workin' this job too, I'm makin' bills, boy. You want me to make a phone call, you need some extra cash before you take off to school, I could make that phone call for you. These niggas got me workin' mad hard. Eight to eight every day, liftin' mad concrete-type shit. 'Cause they buildin' this new jail, right, so they need construction heads, seventeen a hour, kid. I'm makin' bank. .....I don't know what I'ma do next year. I think I'ma start a blunt factory. Nah, I'm playin'. I don't smoke that shit god. .....I don't smoke nothin'. My lungs is pure yo. This the god right here. I'm sayin' how niggas goin' buy into that? Let them white kids smoke them drugs, man. They make that shit. Yeah right, crack also yo. How black people gonna smoke somethin' that's white? You know mad white people be smokin' it too, but you ain't seen them on CNN gettin lifted though.

.....Right, but see, you know what bother me? How one second niggas is like, "Oh yeah, the white man this, white man that." Next second they smokin' Phillies tryin' to watch David Letterman. Explain that. I'm sayin', one second they like, yeah yeah yeah. Next second they like, yeah yeah yeah. You know what I'm sayin'? I'ma tell you like this, Al, it's already 'nuf white kids out here that's tryin' to be black. Peep this, I had to go to Manhattan for this job interview in the Upper West Side. Dead-up word to my moms, I seen this white kid with Filas, Nautica, Philly Blunt shirt, this kid listenin' to X-Clan, walkin' like this . . . [He imitates a white kid imitating a black kid.] What the fuck is this? Nigga look like a Weeble-Wobble and shit. .....Yeah, yeah! But what you call them white people that don't wash theyself, but they be causin' riots and shit? Yeah, them punk-rock anarchy niggas, right? I seen a bunch of them walkin', all raggedy clothes, rings stickin' out they necks and lips. I seen this one black son in there. I said not the god yo. How a brother gonna be in that shit? Know what I'm sayin'?

I be seein' wild shit! I see them on TV, kid! How a sister gonna sing opera? How a black man gonna sing backup for some Kenny G? Kenny Rogers? Any one of them Kenny motherfuckers. They all from Alabama and shit, Kentucky. .....Oh, that's where your school at? For real? . . . I'ma see you at that school yo. I got a scholarship too, son. Government-type shit. They gave me five million dollars, right? They gonna teach me how to make AIDS yo. I'ma make AIDS Two, AIDS Three, AIDS Four, up to Ten. I'ma see how many niggas I could kill yo. Boom! And then 'cause I'ma be rich, right, I'ma buy a penthouse, BMWs, check this yo—I'ma own McDonald's, Nike, Levi's, Sony, all that shit. I'ma own Red Lobster. I'ma own that company that make that bomb that we dropped on that nigga Saddam Hussein family. *Bpow!* I'ma make bank! Then, I'ma see your ass in the street beggin'. You know what I'm sayin', you gonna be beggin'! Talkin' 'bout Frederick Douglass was a great man, lemme get ten cent. And I'ma be like, "Oh whatup, Al, remember me? Remember them college days, this and that?" And I'ma hit you off with a twenty spot 'cause you my boy. I'ma get you a job sweepin' up one of my Red Lobsters. Aha . . .

.....What? .....I'ma do what I want, son, it's a free country, right? .....Oh, oh, you gonna tell a black woman she can't sing opera?! .....A'ight then, a'ight then! He wanna talk garbage right now. This the land of opportunity, son, I ain't tryin' to miss mine yo. This nigga tryin' to keep me down now. You sound like this girl yo. I was tryin' to talk to this girl, she wanna go see this art exhibit, right? So you know me, I got a open mind, right? We step up in this museum. Motherfuckers in suits. And it's this art piece on the wall, it got no frame—nails, glue, and shit is on the wall. Motherfuckers is like, "Mmm, yeah, I like that shit." I said straight up, "That's some bullshit right there." She go like this in my face, son, "Maybe if you was more educated you might understand that." I said,

"What? Hold up now. I'ma go to school so I could understand that shit?" I'ma tell you what, son . . . Nah, I'ma go to school, I'ma be president and I'ma blow niggas' whole countries up all over the earth and I'ma make bank! Understand *that* shit!

.....You see that Lexus right there? That Lexus fat boy. I'ma own Lexus, Jeep . . . Oh shit! I told you I'm gettin' a Jeep? Word to God, kid, red, Cherokee, '91. I'ma have the bomb system in that shit too. Bensi, equalizer . . . 'Cause I had saved up bills from that jail job. Hey yo, seven hundred cells we gonna build in that shit. We gonna lock niggas' heads up all day in that motherfucker, right? So I'm sayin', already I got the Bensi, I got the equalizer. All I got to get is, um, the Jeep, and the insurance. Yo, you should give me your beeper number, we should hang out. .....You don't got a beeper? How somebody supposed to get in touch with you then? .....The phone? Daha. This nigga livin' like Fred Flintstone yo.

On the reals though, I gotta pick up my little brother and get my food. I'ma call you then. .....It's good to see you though, right? Right. Hey yo, Al, they still givin' out applications for that shit that you doin'? I'm sayin' though. Oh, next year? Yeah, I might peep that shit out, definitely though. A'ight then. I'ma call you then. Right. One love god.

[Flex takes a moment and reenters the take-out.] Hey yo, son. Yo, son! Oh, you don't see me now? I said you don't see me right now. You ain't tryin' to serve me now? Never mind, my shit's ready? .....How you know that's mine though? It's in a bag, I can't see that shit. That could be my man's right there. A'ight then, I'ma tell you what, lemme get extra duck sauce, hot sauce, napkins, all that shit, kid. You know extra? Lemme get extra— .....Three twenty-five? . . . Three twenty-five. Don't be tryin' to jerk me neither, man. This nigga tryin to be slick, fuckin' immigrant-ass motherfucker. .....I said you a immigrant. You know what I'm sayin'? You ain't from here, I'm *from* here. Know that shit.

.....How I know what? How I know I'm *from* here? Nigga can't even talk English talkin' 'bout how I know. What you know? You don't know shit! I'm American, son. You ain't shit! Gimme my shit yo. [Flex takes his food and motions to leave but then turns back.] Hey yo, boy, you don't say thank you? Yeah, you're welcome. Know your place yo. I know mine.

PAULA COURT

CÉSAR

[César is fiftyish and is at his first visit to a psychotherapist. He wears a traditional guayabera and hat and carries a cowbell and stick. He sings the first verse of Eddie Palmieri's "Te Palo Pa Rumba" and tries to accompany it with the cowbell.]

... **I DON'T PLAY, I JUST HIT IT.** Because is very difficult if you want to play that. Is not just that you hit it. You have to know what's the rhythm, the music, you have to be musician. Lotta people thinking is just that you hit it. No no. I don't sing also but that song my favorite song. "Te Palo Pa Rumba." The guy who make that song is very famous guy. His name is Eddie Palmieri. That guy, hooh, famous. You ever listen to salsa music? He play piano, and also he tell all the musician what to play. So, if is the trombone, or the trumpet, or the drum or whatever. He gonna explain to them, he's a composer, he compose all the music there. He very famous that guy. .....So you tell me to bring something that I gonna remember what happen, so I bring that [cowbell and stick]. That, I buy to my son when he have only one year old. He never really play because he never listen to salsa music. He only wanna listen to the fast music, I don't know how you call it.

.....Also I bring that [hat]. That I buy to my son when he have ten, eleven years old. He put in the head and he go in the street and he pretend that he Cary Grant. You know Cary Grant? The famous guy? He put in the head for one week and then he throw in the shelf and he never wear. But I keep it because that's my son. So, I supposed to talk to you forty-five minutes, I don't know what you want me to say. .....No, because my wife, she make me come here. Because in my place if you have a problem, you never talking to a therapist. Forget it. In my place if you go to a therapist, they say you crazy in the head. If my friends know I coming here, forget it. They gonna say, "César go crazy." But I trust her. She's very modern, moderna, you know, modern. Very up to date. She reading all the magazine. She gonna look the magazine, then she gonna tell me what I has to do.

Because in my place, if you have a problem, you has to go and talking with un santero o una santera, is like, una consejera. Is a woman, or man, is depend. And she have power, and she take you hand, and she looking you hand, and she tell you what's you problem. Then she tell you you has to take some plant, some herbs, some spices. And you put in the pot. And then you put fire, or some flame there, and you make all the bad thing go out the whole place. Or maybe you put some water, is depend what's you problem.

. . . So my son, he always have a good heart. He never say bad words to nobody, he never punching to nobody. I remember when he have maybe five, six years old. I'm walking to him, with him en the Prospect Park, allá en Brooklyn. And it's the bird. Some bird, the pigeon, is laying in the floor because it's some truck or something gonna come and hit the bird. So the bird laying there in the floor. So my son, he running the bird. He wanna fix it. He say to the bird, "Hey bird, what's the matter with you? You has to get up from there. Is no good that you laying there. You has to go fly . . . up in there." But the bird is only looking in the sky, because the bird know in five minutes, no more. He wanna take the bird home. I say, "You can't take it, the bird is dirty, is from the street." Quería poner como . . . un Band-Aid. But he have a good heart. . . . Maybe when he get a little older, he put some fancy clothes. Not fancy, pero whatever. He put some cologne . . . lotta cologne my son putting there. He go with the girlfriend in the high school. Because he very handsome. He like me, very handsome. I told to my son, "Be careful." Also I told him, "César, I love you." His name is César like my name is César. I make sure I gonna tell him to that.

Because I see in the TV en *Oprah Winfrey,* is some people. They have five kid, three kid, seven kid. Never say I love you. Only they put the hand, throwing out, and what's the kid? Drug, in the street, problems, whatever. Me and my wife, we only having one kid, César. I always making sure I gonna tell to him, "César, I love you." He say to me all the time, "Papi, I know." Because he don't wanna hear. He wanna be man. But I telling that to him anyway.

. . . When he have one year old, I have a big party for him. I invite all the relative from my family, my wife family. They coming all the way from Puerto Rico. Also we have some people from Dominican Republic. New Jersey, Long Island, Connecticut. All coming to my house in New York City for my son gonna have one year old. Almost one hundred people in my house coming. My wife and her sister is cooking. If you ever taste what they cooking that day, you gonna be like, "Oh my God, forget it." It's a lotta dancing in there. It's one place in the party I say to all the people, "Shut up you mouth. Because my son César gonna play 'Te Palo Pa Rumba.' " That song that I told you before. Because that song is come in the Spanish radio station, en esa época when he have one year old. Maybe fifteen, sixteen years ago. Fifteen years.

So I putting him the lap. I put the bell the hand. Because is very heavy, he can't lift it, he only have one year. I put the hand the stick. And everybody is looking. And we play "Te Palo Pa Rumba." The whole song. And it's a long song. And everybody is, "Wow!" I never forget that moment there. Because it's very special to me, that time. That whole time, I taking that time, I put it in here. [He points to his chest.] . . . Four months ago, he come to me, he say, "Papi, I'm going out." I say, "Where you going?" He say, "To the movie." I say, "Okay, be careful." I told him, "César, I love you." He say, "Papi, I know." . . . That's when I lose him. . . . Is very difficult because the police told is some accident that he's running, the police shooting to him but . . . whatever. No because, my wife she working and then she coming home always cry. And I working, and in the night, I never sleep. How I gonna work if I never sleep? She told me, "You better go to sleep." I told her, "Well, you better stop cry entonces." She told me, "César, if you feeling bad, you has to take all the people in the whole world that love you, and you putting those people here [he points to his chest again], and it's gonna making that you feeling warm in here."

So I thinking, "Who love me? My wife love me, put it here. My sister love me, put it here. My two brother love me. . . . My César love me, put it here." And I know that he love me because that day when he go to the movie he say, "Papi, I love you too." It's the only time he say that, but I hear that. Pero very cold in here. . . . I told my wife, "You has to get some better magazine because that's no working." All the time I thinking that he's sitting there and play that, but whatever. I miss him. Maybe I should never coming here, maybe I go talking to some people because maybe you don't listening to me. . . . [César sings the first verse of "Te Palo Pa Rumba" as lights fade out.]

WILL HART

ROUGHNECK CHICKEN

[Epilogue]

[Roughneck Chicken is a mythical character somewhere between Jamaican dub poet, Yiddish sage, and chicken. He wears red, gold, and green and sunglasses. He beats on the wooden cube to provide the music for this poem, which is done in song.]

I HOPE YOU DON'T MIND if I keep you, just a few
likkle minutes after
And if you don't feel like stayin', den get the
hell outta de theatre
But you clap at the end of my show, so I take it
you were listenin'
I hope you have enjoy youself, but listen to this
one more thing
Ey . . .

I know that some of you people have never seen
Brooklyn or Bronx
That's very funny to me, hahahahahahaha
But that's not really the subject of this last and
final part
So let me collect my thoughts together correctly
so that I can start . . .
And remember you came to see theatre, this
ain't no performance art

I want to give you two words, so dat you can
take dem with you

Now don't say dem loud goin' home pon de train, because somebody might hit you
The first word is Dem. That means Dem, those people over there
The second word is We. That means Us, these people over here

Now I hear alotta people talkin', about DemDem, those people and ting,
Dem Terrorist Muslim Crack Addict AIDS Baby Bad Guy Doin' De Tiefin'
Now when I hear people say We, they always feelin' happy
Like We make Three-Billion-Dolla Spaceship, put inna sky, ain't dat nifty?

We make Three Thousand Talk Shows, and the people love it
We kill Three Billion Chickens this year, and make dem inna Chicken Nugget
We made Three Billion Dollars, but We gave money to the poor
We dropped big bombs on those evil fucked-up people and We won the war
Ey . . .

Last month I talk to a Chicken, by the name of Bingi
So pay attention good now, I goin' tell you what the Chicken tole me
Long long time ago . . . Chickens ran de earth
About a Hundred Fifty Thousand Years, before People was birth

The Chickens used to live in big mansions, and the other birds live in the street
The Chickens used to drive BMW, and the other birds walk with dem feet
The Chickens used to say, Look at dem birds, dem filthy lazy bum
How can they live like that really, We are so smart and Dem so dumb

Well today all de Chickens die, and the other birds fly in the sky
That was the end of his story, hahahahahahaha
Ey . . .

Last verse, then you go home . . .

If you don't know my name, me a de Roughneck Chicken, me run de area
And any dibby dibby DJ wan to come try tes me dem ago get murda
I want you to know I am the number one dance-hall chicken inna New York City
And to all de young sexy lady, I want you to know I'm young single and free
So if you want my phone number, well you must come get it from me
Or take youself a visit to Brooklyn, and just ask fe de Dancehall Daddy
Ey . . .

GLOSSARY

A'IGHT: All right.

ASERE: Afro-Cuban for "bro."

BEE: Colloquial for "dude" or "man," as in "What's up, bee . . ." (New York City, U.S.).

BLUNT: A marijuana-filled cigar-leaf cigarette. Derived from Philly Blunts cigars, which were emptied of their tobacco and filled with marijuana.

CLAVE: Musical instrument made of two sticks that are hit together to make a five-beat rhythm called "clave." Used in most forms of Afro-Cuban music; e.g., son, guaguancó, guaracha, rumba, salsa, etc.

FISH: New inmate.

FORTIES: Forty-ounce bottles of malt liquor.

GAT:	Semiautomatic pistol.
GEE:	A thousand dollars; also a colloquialism for "dude" or "guy" (West Coast, U.S.).
GLOCK:	Semiautomatic pistol.
HERB:	An idiot, a sucker.
HO:	Derogatory term for a woman. Derived from "whore"; also a Hip-Hop–derived party exclamation signifying joy or agreement, as in "Everybody say ho! . . ."
LEX:	Lexus automobile.
STEE:	Style. Derived from the Spanish for style— "stilo."
TEC:	Tec-9 automatic machine gun.
TOMMY HIL:	Tommy Hilfiger clothing.
TREY:	Car (West Coast, U.S.).

ABOUT THE AUTHOR

DANNY HOCH's solo show *Some People* won a 1994 OBIE Award at Performance Space 122 and the Joseph Papp Public Theatre (directed by Jo Bonney). *Some People* was filmed for HBO and nominated for a 1996 Cable Ace Award. Danny has toured over thirty-five U.S. cities as well as Austria, Cuba, and Scotland, where he won a Fringe First Award at the Edinburgh Festival. As an actor-teacher, Mr. Hoch spent the first half of this decade bringing conflict-resolution-through-drama to adolescents in New York City's jails and alternative high schools with New York University's Creative Arts Team. A graduate of the High School of Performing Arts in New York City, he also trained at the North Carolina School of the Arts and in London. Mr. Hoch has written and acted for television and in several films, including HBO's *Subway Stories* and Terrence Malick's *Thin Red Line.* His writings have appeared in *Harper's, New Theater Review, American Theatre,* and *Out of Character.* Mr. Hoch is the recipient of a 1994 Solo Theatre Fellowship from the National Endowment for the Arts, a 1996 Sundance Writers Fellowship, a 1998 CalArts/Alpert Award in Theatre, and a 1999 Tennessee Williams Playwrights Fellowship.

Jails, Hospitals & Hip-Hop, Danny Hoch's third solo show, premiered at Berkeley Repertory Theatre in October 1997, where it received a Bay Area Theater Critics Circle Award for Outstanding Solo Performance. In March 1998 *Jails, Hospitals & Hip-Hop* opened in New York City at Performance Space 122, where it was nominated for a 1998 Drama Desk Award, and it was the first off-Broadway production in New York City whose advertising money was spent on Hip-Hop Street Teams and youth ticket subsidies instead of *New York Times* ads. *Jails, Hospitals & Hip-Hop* is being made into a film and will tour twenty cities through the millennium.